ADA CARTIANU

THE NARCISSISM SPECTRUM

AUNVEILING THE TRUTH BEHIND TOXIC RELATIONSHIPS

UNDERSTANDING NARCISSISTIC TYPES AND THEIR IMPACT

Printed in the United States of America

AF722282

THE NARCISSISM SPECTRUM

AUNVEILING THE TRUTH BEHIND
TOXIC RELATIONSHIPS
UNDERSTANDING NARCISSISTIC TYPES
AND THEIR IMPACT

This Book is Informed by a Comprehensive Foundation of Research in Psychology, Clinical Therapy, and Trauma Coaching

---

Our book may be purchased in bulk for educational use.
Please contact your local book seller, Barnes & Noble, Amazon, IngramSpark or Ada Cartianu Art Gallery at
office@adacartianu.com
www.AdaCartianu.com

TABLE OF CONTENTS

Narcissistic abuse can leave you feeling lost in a fog of confusion, but healing is about finding your way back to yourself. It's about rediscovering your voice, your values, and your authentic self.

INTRODUCTION

'The Narcissism Spectrum' is born from personal experience; a journey I wish I hadn't had to take. Through extensive research, clinical therapy, and coaching, I've gained valuable insights that I'm eager to share with others. This book is my way of offering support, considerable knowledge – *knowledge I wish I had before my trauma* – and guidance to those navigating the complexities of narcissistic abuse recovery. It's designed to empower readers to understand what has happened to them, to enable them to heal, to move forward on their journey of recovery, and to build meaningful lives.

Beneath the charming facade, a dangerous game is being played. The narcissist, a master manipulator, wears a mask of confidence and charisma, expertly weaving a web of deceit and emotional manipulation. This book peels back the layers of this deceptive facade, revealing the truth behind the narcissist's mask and empowering you to recognize and navigate the complexities of toxic relationships.

The narcissistic spectrum, a subtle yet insidious force, permeates our social landscape. From the subtle grandiosity of the everyday egotist to the malignant narcissism that wreaks havoc on human lives, the narcissist, in all their guises, poses a profound challenge to the human spirit. This book delves into the intricate tapestry of narcissistic personalities, exploring the diverse manifestations of this complex phenomenon and its profound impact on individuals, relationships, and society as a whole. By understanding the subtle nuances of narcissistic behavior, we can cultivate a deeper awareness of ourselves and others, fostering healthier relationships and navigating the complexities of the human condition with greater wisdom and compassion.

Narcissism is a spectrum, not a single diagnosis. This book explores the various facets of narcissistic behavior, from subtle to overt, and provides readers with the knowledge and tools to recognize and navigate the complexities of toxic relationships.

Love, a sanctuary of intimacy and trust, can become a battlefield when entangled with narcissism. This book delves into the deceptive ways narcissistic personalities infiltrate romantic relationships, leaving a trail of emotional wreckage. From the subtle manipulations to the overt displays of self-absorption, 'The Narcissism Spectrum' provides a nuanced exploration of this complex and often devastating dynamic.

You deserve healthy and fulfilling relationships. This book empowers you to recognize the subtle signs of narcissistic behavior, break free from the cycle of manipulation, and reclaim your power and well-being.

Healing from the trauma of a narcissistic relationship is a journey of self-discovery and empowerment. This book provides a roadmap for navigating the complexities of narcissistic abuse, understanding the impact on your mental and emotional well-being, and ultimately, reclaiming your power and rebuilding your life.

The narcissist's mask conceals a dangerous reality. This book provides the knowledge and tools to recognize the signs, break free from the cycle of manipulation, and heal from the trauma of narcissistic abuse.

Ada Cartianu

To the survivors of narcissistic abuse:
This book is dedicated to you!

May these words offer comfort, support, and the strength to reclaim your power.

This book is dedicated to all who have survived the darkness of abuse. To those still finding their way out, know that healing is possible.

Your journey is unique and valuable, and your voice deserves to be heard.

May this book be a source of strength and hope as you reclaim your power and rebuild your life.

The Narcissist's Mask: Unveiling the Truth Behind Toxic Relationships

UNDERSTANDING NARCISSISM

What is a Narcissist?

A narcissist is often characterized by an inflated sense of self-importance, a deep need for excessive admiration, and a distinct lack of empathy for others. This personality type frequently operates under a veneer of charm and charisma, drawing people in with their magnetic presence. However, beneath this facade lies a complex interplay of insecurity and self-centeredness. Narcissists may exhibit behaviors that can be deeply damaging to those around them, often leaving a trail of emotional turmoil in their wake. Understanding the essence of narcissism is crucial for those who have encountered it, as it paves the way for healing and personal empowerment.

At its core, narcissism can be seen as a defense mechanism, a way for individuals to shield themselves from feelings of inadequacy. This often manifests in grandiose behavior and a constant need for validation. The narcissistic individual may believe they are superior to others, which can lead to manipulative and exploitative behaviors. Recognizing these traits is essential, as it helps victims of narcissistic abuse identify the patterns that may have contributed to their suffering. By understanding that this behavior stems from deep-rooted issues, survivors can begin to detach their self-worth from the narcissist's perception and reclaim their identities.

The impact of narcissistic behavior extends beyond individual relationships; it can profoundly affect family dynamics and broader social circles. Children raised in environments dominated by a narcissistic parent, for example, may struggle with self-esteem issues, emotional regulation, and the ability to form healthy relationships in adulthood. The cycle of abuse often perpetuates itself, as the traits of narcissism can be passed down through generations. Recognizing these patterns is the first step toward breaking the cycle and fostering healthier interactions within families and communities.

Emotional intelligence plays a pivotal role in navigating relationships with narcissistic individuals. It equips individuals with the skills to recognize their emotions, understand the motivations behind the narcissist's behavior, and effectively manage their reactions. By cultivating emotional intelligence, survivors can develop stronger boundaries, enhance their resilience, and foster positive relationships. This growth not only aids in recovery but also empowers individuals to reclaim their narratives and pursue fulfilling connections built on mutual respect and understanding.

The Narcissist's Spectrum: Understanding the Types and Their Impact

THE ESSENCE OF NARCISSISM

Defining Narcissism

Narcissism, at its core, is a complex personality trait marked by an excessive preoccupation with oneself, often at the expense of others' needs and feelings. This self-centeredness manifests in various forms, ranging from overt behaviors such as seeking admiration and attention, to more subtle expressions like emotional manipulation and a profound sense of entitlement. Understanding narcissism is crucial for recognizing its impact on both personal and professional relationships. The spectrum of narcissism encompasses a range of behaviors that can significantly affect the dynamics within families, friendships, and workplaces, highlighting the need for a deeper exploration of its roots and implications.

The main traits that all narcissists have in common include a lack of empathy, an inflated sense of self-importance, and a deep-seated need for validation. These characteristics create a distinctive pattern of behavior that can be damaging to those around them. Narcissists often struggle to form genuine connections, as their worldview is primarily focused on their own desires and achievements. This lack of emotional attunement can lead to toxic relationships, where the needs of others are consistently overlooked. As we delve into the nuances of narcissism, it becomes evident that recognizing these traits is the first step toward protecting oneself and fostering healthier interactions.

Narcissism is not a monolithic condition; it exists on a spectrum with various types, including grandiose, vulnerable, and communal narcissism. Each type exhibits unique traits and behaviors, influencing how individuals engage with others. Grandiose narcissists often display overt confidence and a need for admiration, while vulnerable narcissists may present as insecure and hypersensitive to criticism. Understanding these differences empowers individuals to identify narcissistic behaviors in their lives and navigate the complexities of their interactions with such individuals. This awareness is essential, especially in romantic relationships, where the allure of a charismatic partner can quickly turn into a cycle of emotional turmoil.

In the workplace, narcissism can create challenging dynamics, leading to toxic environments where competition and manipulation thrive. Recognizing narcissistic traits in colleagues or superiors can help individuals establish boundaries and protect their mental well-being.

Similarly, a narcissist parent presents unique challenges, as these individuals may struggle to prioritize the emotional needs of their children. Cultivating an awareness of narcissism's impact on mental health is vital for fostering resilience and promoting healthier relationships. Cultural influences also play a significant role in shaping narcissistic behaviors, highlighting the importance of contextual understanding in addressing this multifaceted issue.

Healing from a relationship with a narcissist requires a profound commitment to self-awareness and growth. Strategies for recovery include establishing boundaries, seeking support from trusted individuals, and engaging in self-reflection. Recognizing the emotional manipulation often employed by narcissists can empower individuals to reclaim their narratives and rebuild their self-esteem. Understanding the distinction between vulnerable and grandiose narcissism further enriches this journey, as it allows for a more nuanced approach to healing and personal development. Ultimately, by fostering awareness and resilience, individuals can navigate the complexities of narcissism and emerge stronger, more empathetic, and better equipped to cultivate fulfilling relationships.

Common Traits of Narcissists

Narcissism is a multifaceted personality trait that manifests in various forms, yet certain common traits unite all narcissists, regardless of their specific type. At the core of narcissism lies an inflated sense of self-importance. This grandiosity often leads individuals to believe they are superior to others, deserving of admiration, and entitled to special treatment. This sense of entitlement can undermine relationships and create challenges in social and professional settings, as narcissists frequently disregard the feelings and needs of those around them. Understanding this trait is crucial for recognizing the impact of narcissism on interpersonal dynamics.

Another defining characteristic of narcissists is their profound need for validation and admiration. They often seek out attention and praise, becoming exceptionally adept at charming others to secure their approval. This relentless pursuit can lead to shallow relationships, as narcissists typically prioritize their own needs over genuine connections. Their constant need for affirmation can create a cycle of emotional manipulation, where they may exploit the vulnerabilities of others to ensure they remain at the center of attention. Recognizing this behavior is essential for anyone navigating a relationship with a narcissist, whether in personal or professional realms.

Emotional instability is also prevalent among narcissists, particularly when their self-image is threatened. They may react with anger, defensiveness, or withdrawal when confronted with criticism or perceived slights. This volatility can create an unpredictable environment, making it challenging for partners, friends, or colleagues to engage with them constructively. Understanding this emotional landscape allows individuals to prepare for and manage interactions with narcissists more effectively, fostering healthier boundaries and reducing the emotional toll of such relationships.

Narcissists often exhibit a lack of empathy, which further distinguishes them from individuals with healthier personality traits. This absence of empathy can lead to significant emotional harm for those in their orbit, as narcissists may struggle to recognize or care for the feelings of others. This trait not only affects romantic relationships but can also permeate workplace dynamics and friendships, leading to a toxic environment. By identifying this characteristic, individuals can better protect themselves and choose relationships that foster mutual respect and understanding.

Lastly, the cultural influences on narcissism cannot be overlooked. In an age where social media often celebrates self-promotion and individualism, narcissistic traits can be inadvertently reinforced. Understanding these cultural dynamics can help adults recognize narcissistic behaviors within themselves and others, facilitating a more profound comprehension of how such traits evolve and manifest. By cultivating awareness and empathy, individuals can strive for healthier relationships and personal growth, freeing themselves from the constraints of narcissistic dynamics and ultimately leading to a more fulfilling life.

The Spectrum of Narcissism

The concept of narcissism exists on a broad spectrum, encompassing a range of behaviors, attitudes, and emotional responses. At one end, we find individuals with grandiose traits, often characterized by an inflated sense of self-importance, a preoccupation with fantasies of unlimited success, and a relentless need for admiration. These individuals can be charming and charismatic, easily drawing people into their orbit. However, their self-centeredness can lead to significant interpersonal conflicts, as they struggle to empathize with others and often exploit relationships for personal gain. Understanding this side of the spectrum is crucial for recognizing the initial allure of narcissistic individuals and the challenges they pose in sustained interactions.

Conversely, the other end of the spectrum features vulnerable narcissists, who may appear shy or insecure yet harbor similar self-centered tendencies. These individuals often oscillate between feelings of inadequacy and a desperate craving for validation. Their narcissism manifests through passive-aggressive behavior, victimhood, and a tendency to manipulate others' emotions to gain sympathy or reassurance. Recognizing these traits is essential, as vulnerable narcissists can be equally damaging in relationships, albeit through more subtle and insidious means. By understanding the duality of narcissism, we can better navigate our interactions and protect ourselves from the emotional turmoil that can arise from both types.

The common traits shared by all narcissists—regardless of their specific type—include a lack of empathy, an excessive need for admiration, and a tendency to manipulate others. These core characteristics create patterns that can profoundly impact romantic relationships, workplace dynamics, and parenting. In romantic contexts, narcissists can create tumultuous relationships marked by emotional highs and lows, leaving partners feeling unvalued and emotionally drained. In the workplace, their drive for power and recognition can foster toxic environments, leading to high employee turnover and low morale. When parenting, narcissistic individuals may prioritize their needs over their children's, potentially stunting emotional development and fostering insecurity in their offspring.

Cultural influences play a significant role in the prevalence and expression of narcissism. In societies that prioritize individualism and success, narcissistic traits may be more likely to thrive, leading to a normalization of self-serving behaviors. This cultural backdrop can complicate our understanding of narcissism, as societal values often blur the lines between healthy self-confidence and pathological narcissism. By examining these cultural factors, we can gain a more profound insight into the roots of narcissistic behaviors and their broader implications for societal health and relationships.

Ultimately, recognizing and understanding the spectrum of narcissism empowers individuals to make informed choices about their relationships. Whether it's identifying narcissistic traits in friends or devising strategies for healing after a relationship with a narcissist, knowledge serves as a protective shield. By fostering awareness and encouraging empathetic connections, we can navigate the complexities of narcissism, creating healthier environments for ourselves and those around us. This journey of understanding is not only about protecting ourselves but also about cultivating compassion for those who struggle with their own narcissistic tendencies, paving the way for healing and growth.

Narcissism: Disorder or Choice?

Narcissism often raises the question of whether it is a psychological disorder or a conscious choice made by individuals. To understand this complex issue, it is essential to delve into the characteristics that define Narcissistic Personality Disorder (NPD) and how these traits manifest in interpersonal relationships. Individuals with narcissistic tendencies may exhibit grandiosity, a profound need for admiration, and a lack of empathy. These traits can lead to toxic dynamics, where the narcissist's behavior causes significant emotional harm to those around them. However, the distinction lies in whether these behaviors stem from an innate disorder or a deliberate decision to engage in harmful patterns.

The debate surrounding narcissism as a disorder or a choice often involves the perspective of emotional intelligence. Those who view narcissism as a disorder argue that individuals with NPD struggle with emotional regulation, often due to underlying trauma or unmet needs from their past. This perspective highlights the importance of compassion and understanding when addressing the actions of narcissists, recognizing that their behavior may be a defense mechanism rather than a calculated choice. In contrast, some believe that narcissism is a conscious choice, where individuals opt to prioritize their needs over the well-being of others, perpetuating cycles of abuse and manipulation.

Navigating relationships with narcissists can be incredibly challenging, especially when considering the impact on emotional health and family dynamics. Toxic relationships often leave deep emotional scars, leading to trauma that may take years to heal. Survivors of narcissistic abuse frequently grapple with feelings of inadequacy, confusion, and betrayal. Understanding the traits of narcissism and identifying red flags can empower individuals to make informed choices about their relationships, ultimately fostering healthier interactions and emotional well-being.

Healing from the trauma of narcissistic abuse requires a multifaceted approach, including building emotional intelligence and developing coping mechanisms. Survivors can benefit from techniques that promote emotional regulation, enabling them to manage their responses to triggers and regain a sense of control. Support systems, such as therapy or support groups, play a crucial role in the recovery journey, providing a safe space to process experiences and share insights. Education about narcissism and its effects on relationships can also empower individuals, raising awareness and encouraging healthy interactions moving forward.

Ultimately, the classification of narcissism as a disorder or a choice invites a deeper exploration of human behavior and the nuances of emotional health. By understanding the underlying factors that contribute to narcissistic traits, individuals can cultivate empathy and compassion for themselves and others. This journey not only aids in personal healing but also encourages the development of positive, nurturing relationships. Empowerment through education and emotional growth helps create a foundation for healthier interactions, fostering resilience in the face of adversity and promoting a brighter future free from the shadows of toxic relationships.

Narcissistic abuse can chip away at your soul,
but you have the power to rebuild,
stronger than before.

TYPES OF NARCISSISTS

• Grandiose Narcissism

Grandiose narcissism stands out as one of the most recognizable forms of narcissistic personality traits, characterized by an inflated sense of self-importance and a deep-seated need for admiration. Individuals exhibiting grandiose narcissism often present themselves as superior to others, displaying an unyielding confidence that can be both captivating and intimidating. Their charm and charisma may draw people in, creating an aura of magnetism that masks the underlying insecurities that fuel their behavior. This facade can lead to a cycle of admiration and validation, where their self-worth is heavily contingent upon the approval of others, often leading to tumultuous relationships and emotional upheaval for those around them.

At the core of grandiose narcissism is a profound lack of empathy, which manifests in their interactions with others. These individuals may exploit relationships to serve their own interests, disregarding the feelings and needs of those they engage with. This characteristic can create significant challenges in romantic relationships, workplace dynamics, and friendships. In romantic partnerships, grandiose narcissists may idealize their partners initially, only to later devalue them when they no longer meet their high expectations. In professional settings, their competitive nature can stifle collaboration and breed resentment among colleagues, ultimately undermining team cohesion and morale.

Understanding grandiose narcissism requires a focus on the broader implications it has on mental health and well-being, both for the narcissist and their loved ones. The relentless pursuit of admiration can lead to cycles of anxiety and depression when their self-image is threatened or when they face criticism. Additionally, those who find themselves entangled in relationships with grandiose narcissists often experience emotional manipulation and a sense of confusion, as their needs and emotions are consistently overlooked. Recognizing these traits is crucial for individuals seeking to protect themselves from emotional harm and to foster healthier relationships.

Cultural influences play a significant role in shaping the prevalence of grandiose narcissism. In societies that emphasize individualism and personal achievement, the traits associated with grandiose narcissism can be more readily accepted or even celebrated. This cultural backdrop can create environments where narcissistic behaviors are reinforced, making it essential for individuals to critically evaluate their interactions and the influence of societal norms on their perceptions of self-worth. Understanding how cultural factors contribute to narcissistic traits can empower individuals to challenge these norms and strive for more authentic connections.

Healing from interactions with grandiose narcissists involves cultivating self-awareness and resilience. By recognizing the patterns of manipulation and emotional detachment, individuals can reclaim their sense of self and establish healthier boundaries. Strategies such as seeking therapy, building supportive relationships, and engaging in self-care practices can foster recovery and personal growth. Ultimately, understanding grandiose narcissism is not only about recognizing its traits but also about empowering oneself to navigate the complexities of relationships, fostering a path toward emotional well-being and healthier interpersonal dynamics.

• Vulnerable Narcissism

Vulnerable narcissism represents a nuanced and often misunderstood segment of the narcissistic spectrum, characterized by an internal struggle that sharply contrasts with the more overt displays of grandiose narcissism. Individuals exhibiting vulnerable narcissistic traits often grapple with feelings of insecurity, inadequacy, and emotional hypersensitivity. While they may not outwardly project the inflated self-esteem typically associated with narcissism, their self-centeredness manifests through a deep need for validation and a tendency to wallow in perceived slights or failures. This internal conflict can create a complex emotional landscape where the need for recognition is intertwined with pervasive feelings of victimization and low self-worth.

At the core of vulnerable narcissism lies an intense fear of rejection and criticism. Unlike their grandiose counterparts, who may flaunt their achievements and demand admiration, vulnerable narcissists often feel like impostors, constantly seeking reassurance from others to counterbalance their fragile self-image. This reliance on external validation can lead to heightened sensitivity to feedback, resulting in defensive reactions when they perceive their worth is being challenged. Understanding this dynamic is crucial for recognizing how vulnerable narcissists may draw others into their emotional turmoil, leading to cycles of dependency and disappointment in relationships.

In romantic relationships, vulnerable narcissists can be particularly challenging partners. Their emotional needs can feel overwhelming, as they oscillate between seeking closeness and pushing others away due to their fears of vulnerability. They may idealize their partners, expecting them to provide constant affirmation and support, which can quickly devolve into feelings of resentment if those needs are not met. This can create a turbulent emotional environment where partners feel as though they are walking on eggshells, trying to navigate the delicate balance between offering support and maintaining their own emotional health.

In the workplace, vulnerable narcissism can manifest as a need for excessive reassurance from colleagues and supervisors. While they may possess capabilities and talents, their fear of inadequacy can hinder their performance and relationships with others. Vulnerable narcissists may engage in passive-aggressive behaviors or become emotionally withdrawn when they feel underappreciated, impacting team dynamics and productivity. It is essential for organizations to foster an environment of open communication and constructive feedback to help mitigate these tendencies and encourage healthier interactions.

Ultimately, understanding vulnerable narcissism allows for a more compassionate perspective on those who exhibit these traits. Recognizing the underlying insecurities and emotional struggles can lead to more effective strategies for interaction and support. For those who find themselves entangled in relationships with vulnerable narcissists, establishing firm boundaries, encouraging open dialogue, and fostering self-care can be vital steps toward emotional healing. By navigating these complexities with awareness and empathy, individuals can create a healthier relational landscape, promoting growth for themselves and those around them.

• Malignant Narcissism

Malignant narcissism represents one of the most destructive forms of narcissism, embodying a blend of narcissistic, antisocial, and paranoid traits that culminate in a deeply ingrained disregard for the well-being of others. Individuals with malignant narcissism not only seek admiration and validation but also exhibit a willingness to exploit and manipulate those around them without remorse. This complex personality type often presents a façade of charm and charisma, drawing others in before revealing their darker motivations. Understanding malignant narcissism is crucial for identifying toxic behaviors and protecting oneself from emotional harm.

At its core, malignant narcissism is characterized by a few key traits that set it apart from other forms of narcissism. These individuals often display a profound need for control, leveraging intimidation and aggression to maintain power over their relationships and environments. Their lack of empathy is striking, as they view others merely as tools for their own gratification. This callousness can result in harmful behaviors that range from emotional abuse to overt manipulation, making it essential for those affected to recognize these traits early on. Being aware of these hallmark characteristics can empower individuals to break free from the malignancy that such personalities impose.

The impact of malignant narcissism extends far into romantic relationships, workplaces, and familial dynamics. In romantic partnerships, malignant narcissists can create cycles of emotional turmoil that leave their partners feeling invalidated and trapped. In the workplace, their manipulative tactics may lead to toxic environments where collaboration and mutual respect are stifled. Parenting dynamics can also be severely affected, as a malignant narcissist may prioritize their own needs over the healthy development of their children, fostering a cycle of dysfunction that can persist for generations. Recognizing these patterns is the first step toward reclaiming one's life and establishing healthier boundaries.

Cultural influences play a significant role in shaping the prevalence and acceptance of narcissistic behaviors. In societies that emphasize individualism and success at any cost, malignant narcissism can thrive, often celebrated in leaders and public figures. This societal backdrop can create an environment where manipulative behaviors are not only tolerated but rewarded, making it even more challenging for individuals to recognize and escape these toxic relationships. By fostering awareness and encouraging open discussions about the implications of such behaviors, communities can work towards reducing the normalization of malignant narcissism.

Healing from the effects of a relationship with a malignant narcissist requires a profound commitment to self-reflection and recovery. Strategies for healing include seeking support from mental health professionals, engaging in self-care practices, and establishing a strong network of understanding friends and family. It is essential for individuals to recognize their worth and rebuild their self-esteem, which can be severely damaged by the insidious nature of narcissistic manipulation. By embracing the journey of healing, victims of malignant narcissism can emerge stronger, more resilient, and equipped to cultivate healthier relationships in the future.

• Covert Narcissism

Covert narcissism, often overshadowed by its more overt counterpart, presents a unique set of challenges for those who encounter it. While grandiose narcissists revel in attention and admiration, covert narcissists often operate in the shadows, exhibiting a more subtle and insidious form of self-absorption. They may appear sensitive, introverted, or even self-effacing, which can mask their deep-seated need for validation and control. This veil of modesty can make them difficult to identify, but understanding their main traits can empower individuals to recognize these behaviors in their relationships, whether personal or professional.

One of the defining characteristics of covert narcissism is a pervasive sense of victimhood. Covert narcissists often view themselves as misunderstood or persecuted, using this narrative to elicit sympathy and manipulate those around them. They may engage in self-pity or passive-aggressive behaviors to draw attention to their struggles while deflecting responsibility for their actions. This dynamic can create an atmosphere of confusion, as their partners or colleagues may find themselves questioning their own perceptions and feelings. By shedding light on these traits, we can better understand the complex dynamics at play in relationships with covert narcissists.

In romantic relationships, covert narcissists can be particularly damaging. They may initially appear charming and attentive, but as the relationship progresses, their need for validation can lead to emotional manipulation and control. They might engage in gaslighting, causing their partners to doubt their own reality, or use guilt as a weapon to maintain dominance. Recognizing these patterns is crucial for anyone navigating a relationship with a covert narcissist, as awareness can foster healthier boundaries and pave the way for emotional recovery.

The impact of covert narcissism extends beyond romantic entanglements; it infiltrates workplaces and family dynamics as well. In professional settings, these individuals may undermine colleagues subtly, using their perceived vulnerability to gain sympathy while simultaneously sabotaging others' work. In parenting, a covert narcissist may place their emotional needs above those of their children, leading to a cycle of neglect and emotional instability. Understanding how covert narcissism manifests in various contexts equips individuals with the tools needed to protect themselves and foster healthier environments.

Ultimately, the journey to healing from the effects of covert narcissism involves recognizing its presence and understanding its implications. By fostering awareness of its traits and behaviors, individuals can better navigate their interactions with covert narcissists, whether in friendships, workplaces, or romantic relationships. Healing begins with acknowledging the emotional toll these relationships can take and seeking support to rebuild self-esteem and emotional resilience. Embracing this path of understanding not only empowers individuals to reclaim their lives but also fosters a greater awareness of the intricate spectrum of narcissism, paving the way for healthier connections and a more compassionate world.

• Communal Narcissism

Communal narcissism represents a unique and often overlooked facet of narcissistic behavior, blending self-interest with a compelling desire to be perceived as altruistic or socially valuable. Unlike traditional narcissists who seek validation through personal achievements or status, communal narcissists derive their self-worth from their perceived contributions to the community or society at large. They thrive on the admiration and recognition of others, positioning themselves as the ultimate helpers, advocates, or caregivers. This form of narcissism can be particularly insidious, as it often masquerades as genuine benevolence, making it challenging to identify and address.

At the core of communal narcissism lies a deep-seated need for validation, which drives these individuals to engage in prosocial behaviors. However, their motivations are often self-serving, as they seek acknowledgment and praise rather than engaging in acts of kindness purely for the sake of helping others. This paradox can create a toxic dynamic in relationships, where the communal narcissist's contributions become a means to an end, overshadowing the genuine needs of those they claim to support. Recognizing these traits is essential, as it allows individuals to navigate interactions with communal narcissists more effectively, establishing boundaries and protecting their own emotional well-being.

In romantic relationships, communal narcissists may initially appear charming and selfless, drawing their partners in with promises of support and understanding. However, over time, their underlying motivations can lead to feelings of inadequacy in their partners, who may feel unworthy of the communal narcissist's affection unless they consistently validate their self-worth. This cycle can be emotionally draining, often resulting in partners feeling more like objects of admiration than true companions. Understanding this dynamic can empower individuals to seek healthier relationships, fostering connections based on mutual respect rather than one-sided admiration.

In the workplace, communal narcissism can manifest as a colleague who takes on excessive responsibilities under the guise of teamwork but ultimately seeks recognition for their efforts. This behavior can create a competitive atmosphere where genuine collaboration is stifled, leading to resentment among coworkers. Moreover, the communal narcissist may manipulate situations to ensure their contributions are highlighted, leaving others feeling undervalued. Recognizing these patterns can help individuals advocate for a more inclusive workplace culture, encouraging authentic collaboration and reducing the impact of narcissistic behaviors on team dynamics.

Ultimately, understanding communal narcissism contributes to a profound comprehension of the broader narcissistic spectrum. By recognizing the traits and behaviors associated with this type, individuals can better navigate their interactions with communal narcissists, whether in personal relationships, professional settings, or within social circles. This awareness fosters resilience, enabling individuals to protect their emotional health and establish boundaries that promote healthier connections. Embracing this knowledge can be a transformative step towards healing and personal growth, allowing individuals to move forward with clarity and strength.

• Overt Narcissism

Overt narcissists are characterized by their grandiose sense of self-importance and a constant need for admiration. They often display an exaggerated belief in their abilities and achievements, seeking to be the center of attention in social and professional environments. This need for recognition can manifest in boasting about their accomplishments or belittling others to elevate their own status. Their overt behavior often results in a lack of empathy, as they prioritize their own needs and desires over those of others. This characteristic can create significant challenges in personal relationships, as overt narcissists tend to disregard the feelings and perspectives of those around them.

In workplace dynamics, overt narcissists can be particularly disruptive. They may engage in manipulative behaviors to climb the corporate ladder, often at the expense of their colleagues. Their self-serving nature can lead to a toxic work environment, where collaboration and teamwork are undermined by their need to assert dominance. These individuals may also engage in public displays of confidence, which can initially impress others but may ultimately lead to resentment. The inability to accept criticism or setbacks can further exacerbate tensions, as overt narcissists often react defensively to any perceived threats to their self-image.

The impact of overt narcissism on relationships is profound and multifaceted. Overt narcissists often struggle to maintain healthy interpersonal connections due to their self-centeredness and lack of emotional support for others. They may engage in constant criticism or manipulation to maintain control in relationships, leading to a cycle of conflict and alienation. Partners, friends, and family members may find themselves feeling invalidated and unappreciated, which can result in emotional distress and, ultimately, the breakdown of these relationships. Understanding these dynamics is crucial for those involved, as it can provide insight into the underlying motivations of the overt narcissist.

Overt narcissism in parenting presents a unique set of challenges for children raised by overt narcissists. These parents often prioritize their own needs and desires over the emotional and developmental needs of their children. This lack of nurturing can lead to children feeling unworthy or emotionally abandoned, which may contribute to long-term psychological issues. The focus on the parent's self-image often overshadows the child's need for love and validation, leading to a cycle of neglect that can perpetuate narcissistic traits in future generations. It is vital to recognize these patterns to break the cycle and promote healthier familial relationships.

Entitlement and self-righteousness are pervasive traits in modern society, particularly among overt narcissists. These individuals often believe they deserve special treatment or recognition, regardless of their actual contributions or merits. This sense of entitlement can lead to conflicts in various social settings, as they may dismiss the achievements of others while expecting admiration and respect for themselves. Generational patterns of narcissism within family systems further complicate this issue, as children of overt narcissists may adopt similar traits, perpetuating a cycle of narcissism. Understanding these dynamics can inform treatment approaches and help identify narcissistic tendencies in social contexts, paving the way for healthier interactions and relationships.

• Antagonistic Narcissism

Antagonistic narcissism is characterized by a distinct blend of self-centeredness and hostility, setting it apart from other narcissistic types. This form of narcissism often manifests in aggressive behavior, a blatant disregard for the feelings of others, and a pronounced need to dominate interpersonal interactions. Individuals exhibiting antagonistic narcissism are not only preoccupied with their own needs but also engage in demeaning and belittling others to elevate their self-esteem. This behavior can create a toxic atmosphere, particularly in workplace dynamics, where such individuals may undermine colleagues and assert their superiority in a manner that is both overt and aggressive.

In relationships, antagonistic narcissism can have devastating effects. Partners of antagonistic narcissists may find themselves in a constant state of emotional turmoil, as these individuals often employ manipulation, intimidation, and verbal abuse to maintain control. The relentless cycle of conflict and emotional volatility can erode trust and intimacy, leading to an environment where love and support are overshadowed by fear and resentment. Understanding the dynamics at play in such relationships is crucial for those seeking to navigate the challenges posed by antagonistic narcissists and to protect their own mental health.

The impact of antagonistic narcissism extends beyond personal relationships and into family dynamics, particularly when it comes to parenting. Parents who display antagonistic traits may prioritize their own needs over those of their children, fostering an environment of neglect or emotional abuse. This can result in children developing their own narcissistic traits or, conversely, struggling with self-esteem issues due to the lack of validation and support. Recognizing the signs of neglectful narcissism in parenting is vital for breaking generational patterns and promoting healthier familial relationships.

Moreover, the interplay of entitlement and self-righteousness often seen in antagonistic narcissists reflects broader societal trends. In modern society, such traits are increasingly prevalent, with individuals feeling justified in their disregard for others in pursuit of personal gain. This societal shift can exacerbate the challenges faced by those affected by narcissistic personalities, as it normalizes behaviors that undermine empathy and cooperation. Addressing these cultural attitudes is essential for fostering a more compassionate community and mitigating the impact of narcissism on interpersonal relationships.

• Neglectful Narcissism

Neglectful narcissists exhibit a unique set of characteristics that can significantly impact their relationships and the environments they inhabit. Unlike overt narcissists, who are often openly grandiose and self-centered, neglectful narcissists tend to be more subtle in their behaviors, often manifesting a profound emotional detachment. This emotional unavailability can create a sense of neglect in their relationships, as they prioritize their own needs and desires over those of others. The result is an insidious form of narcissism that can leave partners, children, and colleagues feeling undervalued and overlooked.

One of the hallmarks of neglectful narcissists is their inability to provide emotional support or validation to those around them. They frequently dismiss the feelings and needs of others, viewing such expressions as unnecessary distractions from their own pursuits. This characteristic can lead to a cycle of emotional neglect, where loved ones may feel compelled to seek validation elsewhere, often leading to feelings of abandonment and worthlessness. In the workplace, these dynamics can manifest as a lack of recognition for team contributions or an unwillingness to mentor or support colleagues, fostering an environment of disengagement and low morale.

Another notable feature of neglectful narcissists is their tendency to evade responsibility for their actions. This avoidance often stems from a deeply ingrained belief that their needs supersede those of others. Consequently, they may deflect blame or minimize the impact of their behavior, which can exacerbate feelings of frustration and resentment among those affected. In family dynamics, this can be particularly damaging, as children raised by neglectful narcissists may struggle with issues of self-esteem and a distorted sense of self-worth, often internalizing the neglect as a reflection of their own inadequacies.

Additionally, neglectful narcissists often exhibit a pattern of inconsistent behavior that can leave others questioning their worth in the relationship. One moment they may appear engaged, while the next, they withdraw emotionally, creating a confusing dynamic for those around them. This inconsistency can lead to a toxic cycle of hope and disappointment, as loved ones strive to earn their attention and affection. In social settings, this unpredictability can manifest as a lack of commitment to friendships or alliances, further isolating the neglectful narcissist from meaningful connections.

Understanding neglectful narcissism is crucial for fostering healthier relationships and addressing the broader implications of this personality type. Recognizing the traits and behaviors associated with neglectful narcissists can help individuals set boundaries and seek support when needed. Moreover, it can aid in developing more effective treatment approaches tailored to this specific type of narcissism, ultimately paving the way for healing and healthier interpersonal dynamics. By unmasking neglectful narcissism, individuals can work toward breaking generational patterns and fostering environments that promote emotional health and connection.

Understanding Neglectful Narcissism in Parenting

Understanding neglectful narcissism in parenting requires a comprehensive examination of how this particular type of narcissism manifests in familial relationships. Neglectful narcissists prioritize their own needs and desires over those of their children, often leading to emotional and psychological harm. Unlike overt narcissists, who may seek constant validation and attention, neglectful narcissists may appear emotionally unavailable, leaving their children feeling invisible and unvalued. This lack of engagement can result in children developing low self-esteem and a skewed perception of love and affection, where they may equate love with neglect or indifference.

Parents exhibiting neglectful narcissism often minimize or dismiss their child's emotional needs. They may fail to provide adequate support during critical developmental stages, leaving children to navigate their feelings alone. This emotional unavailability can manifest in various ways, such as ignoring a child's achievements or being uninterested in their daily experiences. As a result, children may struggle to form healthy relationships later in life, as they often internalize the belief that their feelings and experiences do not matter. This pattern can perpetuate cycles of neglect and emotional unavailability that echo into future generations.

The impact of neglectful narcissism extends beyond childhood, affecting an individual's social and emotional development well into adulthood. Adults raised by neglectful narcissistic parents may find it challenging to assert their needs in relationships, often feeling guilty for wanting attention or support. They may also struggle with feelings of inadequacy, leading to difficulties in forming meaningful connections with others. The ingrained belief that love is conditional or nonexistent can foster anxiety and depression, further complicating their ability to engage in healthy interpersonal dynamics.

In understanding neglectful narcissism, it is essential to recognize the broader cultural implications of this behavior. Societal values that prioritize individual achievement and self-sufficiency can exacerbate the tendencies of neglectful narcissists, promoting an environment where emotional neglect is normalized. This cultural backdrop can create barriers to recognizing and addressing the emotional abuse that arises from neglectful parenting. By acknowledging these societal influences, individuals can begin to reframe their understanding of healthy parenting and the importance of emotional availability in nurturing children.

Addressing the effects of neglectful narcissism in parenting involves both awareness and intervention. Individuals impacted by neglectful narcissistic parents can benefit from therapy and support groups that focus on healing childhood wounds and developing healthy coping strategies. Encouraging self-compassion and fostering emotional intelligence are crucial steps toward breaking the cycle of neglect. By understanding the dynamics of neglectful narcissism, both individuals and society can work towards creating healthier family systems that prioritize emotional connection and support, ultimately promoting well-being across generations.

Long-term Effects on Children

Long-term exposure to various types of narcissism can significantly affect children, shaping their emotional, psychological, and social development in profound ways. Children raised in environments dominated by overt narcissism often struggle with self-esteem issues, as their achievements and worth are frequently measured against unrealistic standards set by their narcissistic parents. The overtly narcissistic parent may demand constant admiration and success, creating a pressure cooker environment where the child feels they must always perform at their best. This relentless pursuit of approval can lead to anxiety, depression, and a pervasive sense of inadequacy, as the child internalizes the belief that they are never good enough.

Neglectful narcissism introduces a different set of challenges. Children in these environments often experience emotional volatility and conflict, as antagonistic narcissists tend to engage in manipulative or aggressive behaviors. Such an upbringing can normalize toxic conflict, making it difficult for children to form healthy relationships later in life. They may struggle with trust issues, as they have learned to expect betrayal or hostility rather than support and affection. This can lead to a pattern of dysfunctional relationships in adulthood, as they may either replicate the conflicts they witnessed or become overly accommodating to avoid confrontation.

Neglectful narcissism presents another layer of complexity. In these scenarios, the child may receive little to no emotional support or validation, as the parent prioritizes their own needs and desires over those of the child. The long-term effects can be devastating, leading to feelings of worthlessness and abandonment. Children raised in neglectful environments often struggle to understand their own emotions, leading to difficulties in expressing themselves and forming attachments. They may become adults who either withdraw from relationships entirely or seek out unhealthy connections in a desperate attempt to find the validation they lacked in childhood.

Entitlement and self-righteousness, prevalent in some narcissistic parents, can instill a skewed worldview in children. They may develop a sense of superiority and an expectation that they deserve preferential treatment in all aspects of life. This can manifest in various social settings, where they may struggle to empathize with others or accept differing viewpoints. As adults, these individuals might find themselves alienated from peers, unable to maintain friendships or professional relationships due to their inflated sense of self and disregard for others' feelings and contributions.

Generational patterns of narcissism in family systems can perpetuate these issues, creating a cycle that is difficult to break. Children who witness narcissistic behaviors often repeat these patterns in their own parenting, perpetuating the cycle of emotional neglect or abuse. Understanding these long-term effects is crucial for adults who may have experienced such dynamics, as it allows for the identification of narcissistic traits within themselves and others. By recognizing these patterns, individuals can seek appropriate treatment approaches and work towards healthier relationships, ultimately breaking the generational cycle of narcissism and fostering a more nurturing environment for future generations.

• Benign Narcissism

Benign narcissists exhibit a unique blend of self-centeredness and an outwardly pleasant demeanor, often making them more socially acceptable than their overt or antagonistic counterparts. They tend to possess an inflated sense of self-importance but express it in ways that can be perceived as charming or likable. This type of narcissist often seeks attention and validation but does so in a manner that minimizes direct conflict, leading others to overlook or excuse their self-serving behaviors. In social settings, benign narcissists can come across as charismatic, drawing people in with their engaging personalities while simultaneously prioritizing their own needs and desires.

One of the defining traits of benign narcissists is their ability to maintain a facade of empathy and concern for others, which can mask their underlying self-absorption. Unlike overt narcissists who often flaunt their superiority, benign narcissists may demonstrate a superficial understanding of empathy, using it as a tool to further their own agendas. They may engage in acts of kindness or support, but these actions are frequently motivated by the desire for admiration and recognition rather than genuine altruism. This can create a complex dynamic in relationships, where others are often left feeling confused about the true nature of their intentions.

In workplace dynamics, benign narcissists can be particularly challenging to identify. They often occupy roles where they can shine, such as leadership positions or public-facing jobs, leveraging their charm to build a favorable image. Their desire for admiration may drive them to seek validation through accomplishments or recognition, which can motivate them to perform well. However, this same trait can lead to a lack of accountability, as they may deflect criticism and fail to acknowledge the contributions of others. Consequently, colleagues may find themselves caught in a cycle of supporting and validating the benign narcissist while their own needs go unmet.

The impact of benign narcissism on interpersonal relationships can be subtle yet profound. Partners and friends may initially feel uplifted by the benign narcissist's charisma and enthusiasm, only to later realize that their emotional needs are often sidelined. The benign narcissist's need for admiration can create an imbalance in the relationship, where the focus tends to be on their desires and achievements, leaving others feeling undervalued. Over time, this dynamic can lead to resentment and emotional distance, as those close to the benign narcissist struggle to assert their own needs in the relationship.

Understanding benign narcissists involves recognizing the interplay between their charming exterior and their underlying self-centeredness. While they may not exhibit the overtly harmful behaviors associated with other narcissistic types, their impact on social and relational dynamics can be significant. Identifying the traits of benign narcissists is crucial for maintaining healthy relationships. By fostering awareness of these behaviors, individuals can navigate their interactions more effectively, setting boundaries to ensure their emotional needs are met while also managing the complexities that arise from engaging with someone who embodies the traits of benign narcissism.

ENTITLEMENT AND SELF-RIGHTEOUSNESS

Understanding Entitlement in Society

Entitlement in society manifests as an expectation that one deserves certain privileges or treatment without corresponding responsibilities. This mindset is often rooted in narcissistic traits, where individuals perceive themselves as superior and deserving of special consideration. Overt narcissists, for instance, may openly express their entitlement, demanding recognition and admiration from others. This behavior can lead to significant disruption in social and professional settings, as their inflated sense of self-worth often disregards the needs and rights of those around them. Understanding the dynamics of entitlement is crucial in recognizing how it influences relationships and workplace interactions.

In the context of workplace dynamics, overt narcissists can create toxic environments. Their entitlement often leads to a lack of accountability, as they believe their contributions should be valued above others. This self-centered perspective can breed resentment among colleagues and foster a culture of competition rather than collaboration. Antagonistic narcissists, while similarly entitled, may express their superiority through hostility and aggression. Their need to assert dominance can further complicate workplace relationships, making it essential for organizations to implement strategies that mitigate the impact of these narcissistic behaviors.

The concept of entitlement extends beyond the workplace and infiltrates personal relationships, particularly in parenting. Neglectful narcissism, characterized by emotional unavailability and a lack of nurturing, can result in children developing their own sense of entitlement as a coping mechanism. These children may grow up believing they are deserving of attention and validation without having to reciprocate. As they navigate adulthood, this ingrained mindset can lead to dysfunctional relationships and a failure to establish healthy boundaries, perpetuating a cycle of narcissism within family systems.

Entitlement and self-righteousness are also prevalent themes in modern society, where cultural narratives often reinforce the idea that individuals deserve certain outcomes despite their actions. This societal inclination can amplify narcissistic traits, as people increasingly prioritize their desires over communal well-being. Generational patterns of narcissism reveal how entitlement can be passed down, with parents modeling these behaviors that children internalize. Understanding these dynamics is vital for breaking the cycle and fostering healthier interactions both within families and the broader community.

Addressing entitlement in the context of narcissism requires thoughtful intervention and treatment approaches tailored to the specific narcissistic types. Therapy can help individuals recognize their entitlement and its impact on relationships, encouraging the development of empathy and accountability. Identifying narcissistic traits in social settings can also empower individuals to set boundaries and seek healthier connections. By unmasking the underlying entitlement issues associated with various forms of narcissism, society can work towards fostering a more compassionate and equitable environment for all.

Self-Righteousness as a Narcissistic Trait

Self-righteousness manifests as a prominent trait among various narcissistic types, particularly in overt and entitled narcissists. This self-righteousness stems from an inflated sense of superiority and an unwavering belief in one's moral or ethical standing. Such individuals often view themselves as paragons of virtue, leading them to judge others harshly. This judgmental lens not only serves to elevate their self-image but also diminishes the worth of those around them. In social and workplace settings, this trait can create a toxic environment where individuals feel belittled and undervalued, leading to strained relationships and decreased morale.

In the workplace, self-righteous overt narcissists may position themselves as the moral compass of the team. They often exhibit a need to be seen as the ultimate authority on ethical matters, using their self-proclaimed superiority to dominate discussions and decision-making processes. This behavior can stifle collaboration and discourage open dialogue, as team members may feel intimidated or invalidated. The impact of such dynamics can ripple through the organization, resulting in diminished productivity and increased turnover. Recognizing this trait is crucial for fostering a healthy workplace culture that values diverse perspectives and encourages mutual respect.

Antagonistic narcissists also exhibit self-righteousness, but their approach is more confrontational and aggressive. They often engage in moral grandstanding, using public displays of outrage to assert their superiority. This behavior can alienate peers and create a hostile environment where conflict thrives. In personal relationships, self-righteous antagonistic narcissists may manipulate situations to cast themselves as the victim, further entrenching their moral high ground. This tactic not only reinforces their self-image but also complicates the emotional landscape for those involved, leading to increased tension and unresolved conflict.

Neglectful narcissists, while less overtly self-righteous, often exhibit this trait through passive-aggressive behavior. Their indifference towards others can be perceived as a subtle form of judgment, as they prioritize their needs over the emotional well-being of those around them. This neglect can foster feelings of inadequacy in others, reinforcing the neglectful narcissist's inflated self-image. Understanding self-righteousness in this context is essential for recognizing the subtle, yet damaging, effects of neglectful behavior on family dynamics and personal relationships.

Addressing self-righteousness as a narcissistic trait requires a nuanced understanding of its roots and manifestations. Treatment approaches for narcissistic individuals often involve cognitive behavioral therapy and other interventions aimed at fostering empathy and self-awareness. By unpacking the self-righteous narratives that fuel their behavior, individuals can begin to recognize the impact of their actions on others. This process not only aids in personal growth but also contributes to healthier relationships and a more compassionate society, challenging the entitlement that often accompanies self-righteousness in modern culture.

Implications for Social Interactions

Understanding the implications of various narcissistic types on social interactions is crucial for navigating personal and professional relationships. Overt narcissists, characterized by their grandiosity and need for admiration, often dominate social settings. Their self-centered nature can lead to an environment where others feel overshadowed or dismissed. This behavior can manifest in workplace dynamics, where overt narcissists may take credit for team achievements or disregard colleagues' contributions. The impact on group morale can be significant, leading to resentment and a lack of collaboration, ultimately hindering productivity and creativity.

Antagonistic narcissists take social interactions a step further by displaying hostility and aggression. Their interactions are often laced with criticism and manipulation, creating a toxic atmosphere that can alienate peers and loved ones. In personal relationships, this type can lead to cycles of conflict and emotional exhaustion, as their partners may feel compelled to defend themselves against unwarranted attacks. The inability to engage in healthy dialogue further exacerbates these dynamics, leaving individuals feeling isolated and unsupported. Recognizing these patterns is essential for anyone seeking to maintain their mental health in the face of antagonistic behavior.

Neglectful narcissism, particularly in parenting, has profound implications for children's social development. Parents exhibiting neglectful narcissism may prioritize their own needs over those of their children, resulting in emotional unavailability. Children raised in such environments may struggle with self-esteem and social skills, as they have not received the necessary emotional support to develop healthy interpersonal relationships. The long-term effects can manifest as difficulties in forming secure attachments, leading to patterns of relationship dysfunction in adulthood. Understanding these dynamics is vital for breaking the cycle of neglect and fostering healthier family interactions.

Entitlement and self-righteousness have become increasingly prevalent in modern society, influencing social interactions at every level. Individuals displaying these traits often view themselves as deserving of special treatment, which can lead to friction in both personal and professional realms. This sense of superiority can alienate peers and create an environment of tension and competition, rather than cooperation. The implications of this behavior extend beyond the individual, affecting group cohesion and societal norms. Raising awareness about these traits can encourage individuals to reflect on their behaviors and foster a more empathetic community.

THE PROFOUND NATURE OF NARCISSISM

Historical Perspectives on Narcissism

From ancient myths to modern society, historical perspectives on narcissism offer a multifaceted view of this complex and enduring human trait, its manifestations evolving and intertwining throughout time. Ancient mythology first introduced the concept through the tale of Narcissus, a figure who became so enamored with his own reflection that he lost sight of reality. This myth serves as a powerful metaphor for the self-absorption and vanity that characterize narcissism. As societies progressed, philosophers and psychologists began to explore these traits more deeply, with figures such as Sigmund Freud highlighting the interplay between narcissism and human development, recognizing its dual nature as both a potential source of creativity and a barrier to genuine connection.

The 20th century marked a significant shift in the perception of narcissism, particularly as the field of psychology expanded. The emergence of psychoanalytic theories provided a framework for understanding narcissistic behaviors beyond mere vanity. Researchers like Heinz Kohut emphasized the developmental aspects of narcissism, illustrating how early childhood experiences shape one's self-image and interpersonal relationships. This perspective laid the groundwork for distinguishing between various types of narcissism, such as grandiose and vulnerable, enriching our comprehension of how these traits manifest in individuals and impact their interactions with others.

As the 21st century dawned, cultural influences began to play a pivotal role in shaping perceptions of narcissism. The rise of social media and a culture of self-promotion has led to an environment where narcissistic traits can flourish. This phenomenon has sparked debates about the normalization of self-centered behavior and its implications for mental health and relationships. Understanding the historical context of narcissism allows us to critically evaluate these cultural shifts, helping us discern where healthy self-esteem ends and pathological narcissism begins.

Narcissism's impact extends into various facets of life, including romantic relationships, workplaces, and parenting. Historical analysis sheds light on how different eras have approached these dynamics, revealing patterns that resonate today. In romantic contexts, narcissists often engage in emotional manipulation, creating toxic cycles that can leave partners feeling diminished. Likewise, in professional environments, the presence of narcissistic individuals can disrupt team cohesion and productivity. Recognizing these patterns is essential for fostering healthier interactions and creating boundaries that protect one's well-being.

The journey of understanding narcissism is ongoing, yet the historical perspectives provide invaluable insights. By examining how perceptions have evolved, we can better navigate the challenges posed by narcissistic individuals in our lives. Whether recognizing traits in friends, understanding the nuances of parenting a narcissist, or healing after a damaging relationship, these insights empower us to foster resilience and cultivate healthier connections. Embracing this knowledge can lead to a profound understanding of ourselves and others, guiding us toward more fulfilling relationships free from the shadows of narcissism.

Psychological Underpinnings

The psychological underpinnings of narcissism reveal a complex tapestry woven from a blend of childhood experiences, personality traits, and societal influences. At the core of narcissistic behavior lies a fragile self-esteem, often masked by an inflated sense of self-importance. This dichotomy leads to the emergence of common traits among narcissists, including a profound need for admiration, a lack of empathy, and a tendency to exploit relationships for personal gain. Understanding these traits is essential for adults navigating their interactions with narcissistic individuals, whether in romantic relationships, workplaces, or even within familial structures.

Delving into the types of narcissists provides deeper insights into their behaviors and motivations. Grandiose narcissists display overt arrogance and a sense of superiority, often thriving on attention and validation. In contrast, vulnerable narcissists may present as sensitive and insecure, yet they harbor a deep-seated need for affirmation and recognition. Recognizing these distinctions can empower individuals to identify the narcissistic dynamics at play in their lives, allowing for more informed coping strategies. This understanding paves the way for personal growth, as it encourages adults to reassess their boundaries and emotional investments in potentially toxic relationships.

The impact of narcissism extends beyond individual relationships and seeps into broader social contexts, including workplace environments and parenting styles. In the workplace, narcissistic colleagues or leaders may disrupt team dynamics, fostering an atmosphere of competition rather than collaboration. Similarly, parenting a narcissist can perpetuate cycles of emotional manipulation and neglect, affecting not only the narcissist but also the children caught in their orbit. Recognizing these patterns is crucial for adults aiming to cultivate healthier environments, whether at home or in professional settings.

It is important to understand that societal values that prioritize individualism, success, and surface-level achievements can exacerbate narcissistic tendencies. Adults are encouraged to critically evaluate these cultural narratives and their personal implications, fostering a more compassionate understanding of themselves and others. This reflection can lead to a collective effort to combat narcissism, promoting empathy and connection in a world that often encourages disconnection.

Healing after a relationship with a narcissist requires profound self-reflection and resilience. Adults must navigate the emotional fallout, learning to recognize and reclaim their self-worth in the aftermath of manipulation. Strategies for healing may include seeking support from trusted friends, engaging in therapy, and practicing self-compassion. By understanding the psychological underpinnings of narcissism, individuals can not only break free from toxic relationships but also emerge stronger, more self-aware, and equipped to foster healthier connections in their lives.

VULNERABLE VS. GRANDIOSE NARCISSISM

• Defining Vulnerable Narcissism

Vulnerable narcissism represents a complex and often misunderstood aspect of the broader narcissistic spectrum. Unlike its more overt counterpart, grandiose narcissism, vulnerable narcissism is characterized by an inner sense of insecurity and fragility. Those who exhibit this form of narcissism may appear shy, sensitive, or even self-effacing, yet they harbor deep-seated feelings of entitlement and a need for validation. This paradox can leave them feeling isolated, as they oscillate between seeking admiration and retreating into their vulnerabilities. Understanding vulnerable narcissism is essential for recognizing the various ways narcissistic traits manifest in relationships and daily life.

At the core of vulnerable narcissism lies a profound fear of rejection and inadequacy. Individuals with these traits often have a heightened sensitivity to criticism and may react defensively when they perceive threats to their self-worth. This sensitivity can lead to emotional manipulation, where they evoke sympathy or guilt from others to maintain their perceived value. Their need for reassurance can become overwhelming, creating a cycle where their relationships are fraught with tension and emotional volatility. Recognizing this pattern is crucial for both the vulnerable narcissist and those in their orbit, as it allows for healthier interactions and boundaries.

In romantic relationships, vulnerable narcissists may initially be presented as deeply caring and attentive partners, drawing others in with their emotional depth. However, as the relationship progresses, their insecurities may surface, leading to behaviors that can be damaging. They may alternate between idealization and devaluation, leaving partners feeling confused and emotionally drained. Understanding these dynamics can empower individuals to navigate relationships with vulnerable narcissists more effectively, fostering an environment where open communication and mutual respect can thrive.

The impact of vulnerable narcissism extends beyond personal relationships into the workplace and parenting. In a professional setting, vulnerable narcissists might struggle with authority and collaboration, often feeling threatened by peers. Their need for validation can lead to passive-aggressive behavior or withdrawal, undermining team dynamics. As parents, those with vulnerable narcissistic traits may unintentionally pass on their insecurities to their children, fostering cycles of emotional dependency and low self-esteem. Recognizing these patterns can help break the cycle, allowing individuals to foster healthier environments for themselves and those around them.

Ultimately, understanding vulnerable narcissism is a pathway to healing and growth, both for those who exhibit these traits and for those affected by them. By recognizing the signs and underlying motivations, individuals can cultivate empathy and compassion, paving the way for healthier relationships. This understanding can also serve as a guide for personal development, encouraging vulnerable narcissists to confront their insecurities and seek fulfillment from within rather than relying on external validation. In doing so, they can break free from the constraints of their vulnerabilities and foster deeper, more meaningful connections with others.

• Defining Grandiose Narcissism

Grandiose narcissism represents a striking manifestation of narcissistic traits, characterized by an inflated sense of self-importance, an overwhelming need for admiration, and a lack of empathy. Individuals exhibiting this type of narcissism often present themselves as superior to others, believing they are unique and deserving of special treatment. This grandiosity can manifest in various ways, from boastful behavior and excessive confidence to a relentless pursuit of success and recognition. These individuals may often dominate conversations, seeking to be the center of attention, and can display a deep-seated belief that they are entitled to the best of everything, be it in their careers, relationships, or social standings.

At the core of grandiose narcissism lies a fragile self-esteem that requires constant reinforcement through external validation. While these individuals may appear self-assured, their self-worth is precariously balanced on the admiration they receive from others. This need for validation can lead to a cycle of seeking accolades and accolades, resulting in superficial relationships that lack depth and sincerity. In romantic contexts, grandiose narcissists can be particularly challenging, as their self-centeredness often eclipses their partner's needs and desires, leading to emotional turmoil and unbalanced dynamics. Understanding this trait is vital for anyone navigating relationships with such individuals, as it provides insights into their behavior and motivations.

Recognizing grandiose narcissism is essential not only for personal relationships but also for professional environments. In the workplace, grandiose narcissists can be incredibly charismatic and persuasive, often rising to leadership positions where their ambitious nature shines. However, their lack of empathy can create toxic work environments, as they may exploit or manipulate colleagues to achieve their goals. This behavior can lead to significant challenges for teams, as collaboration and mutual respect are sacrificed for personal gain. Acknowledging these traits can empower individuals and organizations to develop strategies that mitigate the negative impacts of such personalities on workplace dynamics.

Culturally, grandiose narcissism is often reinforced by societal values that prioritize individual success and achievement. In environments that glorify competition and personal branding, individuals may feel compelled to adopt narcissistic traits to thrive. This cultural backdrop can further complicate the understanding of narcissism, blurring the lines between healthy self-confidence and destructive grandiosity. By fostering awareness of these influences, individuals can cultivate healthier perspectives on self-worth and success, ultimately leading to more authentic connections with others.

Navigating relationships with grandiose narcissists requires a profound understanding of their traits and patterns. It is crucial to establish boundaries and recognize when manipulation occurs. For those seeking healing after interactions with such individuals, fostering self-compassion and building a supportive network can be instrumental. Embracing one's own worth, independent of external validation, serves as a powerful antidote to the emotional turmoil often caused by grandiose narcissism. By cultivating resilience and self-awareness, individuals can reclaim their sense of self and move forward with confidence, free from the shadows of narcissistic influence.

The Impact of Both Types on Relationships

The impact of both vulnerable and grandiose narcissism on relationships is profound and multifaceted. Each type of narcissist brings unique challenges and dynamics that can significantly affect interpersonal connections. While grandiose narcissists often exhibit overt charisma and confidence, their need for admiration and lack of empathy can lead to superficial relationships. In contrast, vulnerable narcissists may present as insecure and fragile, yet their profound self-centeredness can create a toxic environment that stifles genuine intimacy. Understanding these distinctions is crucial for individuals seeking to navigate their relationships with narcissists, whether in romantic contexts, workplaces, or friendships.

In romantic relationships, the grandiose narcissist often captivates their partner with charm and intensity, creating an initial allure that feels intoxicating. However, as the relationship unfolds, the partner may find themselves on an emotional roller coaster, constantly seeking validation while grappling with the grandiose narcissist's demands for attention. The partner's self-worth can diminish as they become increasingly enmeshed in the narcissist's world, where their needs are secondary. On the other hand, vulnerable narcissists may elicit feelings of concern and protectiveness from their partners, but this dynamic can quickly shift into a cycle of emotional manipulation and guilt, leaving the partner feeling drained and unfulfilled.

In the workplace, both types of narcissists can create an environment rife with tension and competition. Grandiose narcissists often seek positions of power and can undermine colleagues to establish dominance. Their tendency to take credit for others' work and their lack of accountability can lead to a toxic culture, fostering resentment among team members. Vulnerable narcissists, while perhaps less overtly aggressive, can create conflict through passive-aggressive behaviors and an overwhelming need for reassurance. Both types can disrupt teamwork and collaboration, highlighting the necessity for awareness and strategies to mitigate their influence in professional settings.

Having a narcissistic parent also presents unique challenges, particularly when considering the emotional development of children. Grandiose narcissistic parents may prioritize their own needs and achievements, imparting a sense of entitlement to their children while neglecting their emotional well-being. Conversely, vulnerable narcissistic parents might project their insecurities onto their children, leading to an environment where the child feels responsible for the parent's emotional state. Such dynamics can create lasting impacts on a child's self-esteem and relational patterns, necessitating a deeper understanding of the narcissistic traits exhibited by parents and their implications on future relationships.

Recognizing the differences between vulnerable and grandiose narcissism is vital for fostering healthier relationships. By understanding these dynamics, individuals can learn to set boundaries, seek support, and prioritize their own well-being. Healing from relationships with narcissists—whether they are friends, partners, or family members—requires a commitment to self-reflection and growth. As adults navigate the complexities of their connections, a profound understanding of narcissism enables them to cultivate healthier interactions, break free from toxic patterns, and embrace relationships that nurture rather than depleting their emotional resources.

NARCISSISM AND EMOTIONAL MANIPULATION

Understanding Manipulative Behaviors

Understanding manipulative behaviors is crucial for anyone seeking to navigate the complex terrain of relationships impacted by narcissism. At the heart of manipulation lies a desire for control, often manifested through deceit, emotional exploitation, and a lack of empathy. Recognizing these behaviors is the first step toward empowering oneself and others. Manipulative individuals, particularly those on the narcissistic spectrum, employ tactics such as gaslighting, guilt-tripping, and love-bombing, which can distort reality and undermine confidence. Understanding these tactics allows individuals to reclaim their narrative and foster healthier interactions.

Narcissists often share common traits that make their manipulative behaviors particularly insidious. They may possess an inflated sense of self-importance, a deep need for admiration, and a remarkable ability to charm and disarm those around them. However, beneath this veneer lies an emotional fragility that drives their need to manipulate. By analyzing these traits, one can begin to see through the façade and recognize the underlying motivations that fuel harmful behaviors. This awareness can be liberating, as it enables individuals to set clear boundaries and protect their emotional well-being.

The different types of narcissists further complicate the landscape of manipulation. From grandiose narcissists, who are overt in their self-aggrandizement, to vulnerable narcissists, who may present as insecure yet still manipulate through emotional dependence, understanding these variations can enhance our ability to navigate relationships. Each type employs distinct strategies to maintain their self-image and exert control over others. By identifying the type of narcissism at play, individuals can tailor their responses and strategies for disengagement, leading to healthier and more fulfilling relationships.

Navigating narcissism in romantic relationships or the workplace introduces a unique set of challenges that often involve emotional manipulation. In romantic settings, a partner may use manipulation to create dependency or undermine the other's self-esteem. In the workplace, the stakes can be equally high, with narcissistic colleagues or bosses engaging in power plays that may stifle creativity and collaboration. Recognizing these patterns is essential for maintaining one's integrity and ensuring that one does not become ensnared in a web of manipulation. This awareness fosters resilience, allowing individuals to assert their rights and advocate for themselves.

Cultural influences also play a significant role in shaping how narcissism and manipulative behaviors manifest. In societies that prioritize individual achievement and status, narcissistic traits may be more normalized, leading to an increase in manipulative behaviors across various contexts. By understanding these cultural dimensions, one can better contextualize their experiences and develop strategies for healing and growth after encountering a narcissistic individual. Embracing this knowledge equips individuals with the tools needed to break free from harmful dynamics and pursue healthier, more authentic connections that celebrate mutual respect and understanding.

Recognizing Gaslighting

Recognizing gaslighting is a crucial step in navigating the complex landscape of narcissism. Gaslighting, a term derived from the

1944 film "Gaslight," involves subtle manipulations that make individuals question their reality, memory, and even their sanity. This insidious form of emotional abuse is often employed by narcissists as a means to exert control over their victims. By understanding the signs of gaslighting, adults can begin to reclaim their reality and protect themselves from the damaging effects of this form of manipulation.

One of the most telling signs of gaslighting is the consistent denial of facts or events. A narcissist may dismiss your recollections or feelings as exaggerated, irrational, or even nonexistent. This persistent invalidation can leave you feeling confused and uncertain. Recognizing this pattern is essential; when you start to doubt your perceptions and memories, it's a clear indication that gaslighting is at play. It is vital to trust your instincts and document your experiences, as this can serve as a grounding tool when faced with the relentless distortion of truth.

Another hallmark of gaslighting is the use of blame to shift responsibility. A narcissistic individual may twist situations to make you feel guilty or responsible for their actions, creating a cycle of self-doubt. They may say things like, "If you hadn't reacted that way, I wouldn't have done this." Understanding that this tactic is a deliberate manipulation can empower you to break free from the cycle of blame. By recognizing that their behavior stems from their own insecurities, you can strengthen your resolve to stand firm in your truth.

Emotional manipulation often accompanies gaslighting, manifesting through constant comparisons or belittling remarks. A narcissist may highlight your flaws while praising others, fostering an environment of insecurity. This tactic not only reinforces their superiority but also keeps you trapped in a cycle of self-criticism and confusion. By becoming aware of these manipulative behaviors, you can cultivate self-compassion and seek support from trusted friends or professionals who can help you re-establish a healthy self-image.

Recognizing gaslighting is not just about identifying harmful behaviors; it's about reclaiming your narrative and your power. Understanding the dynamics of narcissism equips you with the tools to protect yourself from emotional manipulation. By setting boundaries and seeking support, you can move toward healing and empowerment. Remember, you have the right to your feelings and experiences. By acknowledging and confronting gaslighting, you can pave the way for healthier relationships and a more authentic life.

Protecting Yourself

Protecting yourself from the influence of narcissists is crucial in navigating relationships, whether they are romantic, professional, or familial. Understanding the traits that define narcissism is the first step toward establishing healthy boundaries. Recognizing these traits in others allows you to identify potential threats to your emotional well-being. Key characteristics such as lack of empathy, an inflated sense of self-importance, and manipulative behavior often manifest in various forms, making it essential to remain vigilant. By educating yourself about these behaviors, you empower yourself to make informed decisions about whom to engage with and how to protect your emotional health.

Creating and maintaining boundaries is vital when dealing with narcissists. It is important to establish clear limits regarding acceptable behavior and to communicate these boundaries assertively. Narcissists often test limits, seeking to undermine your confidence or manipulate your emotions. By standing firm in your boundaries, you not only defend your mental space but also signal to the narcissist that their tactics will not be tolerated. This act of self-assertion is a powerful form of self-protection and serves as a reminder that you deserve respect and kindness in all your relationships.

Another key aspect of protecting yourself involves fostering a support system of trusted friends and family. Surrounding yourself with empathetic and understanding individuals can serve as a buffer against the emotional turmoil that a narcissistic person may create. These allies can provide perspective, validation, and encouragement when you feel overwhelmed or manipulated. Their support can help you rebuild your self-esteem and reinforce your understanding of healthy relationships. Remember, you do not have to navigate the complexities of narcissistic dynamics alone; a strong support network can be your greatest asset.

Furthermore, it is crucial to prioritize self-care and emotional health when dealing with narcissistic individuals. Engaging in activities that nurture your well-being, such as mindfulness, therapy, or creative pursuits, can help you regain a sense of control and peace. These practices allow you to process your feelings and reinforce your identity outside of the narcissist's influence. By investing in your personal growth, you become more resilient and self-aware, making it easier to recognize red flags in future relationships.

Lastly, understanding the different types of narcissists—whether grandiose or vulnerable—can enhance your ability to protect yourself. Each type may employ different manipulation strategies, and recognizing these can help you anticipate their actions. This knowledge not only enables you to navigate interactions with greater insight but also aids in crafting effective responses. Ultimately, arming yourself with understanding, boundaries, support, and self-care strategies creates a robust defense against the detrimental effects of narcissistic relationships, allowing you to reclaim your power and foster healthier connections.

Symptoms and Diagnosis of Narcissistic Personality Disorder

Narcissistic Personality Disorder (NPD) manifests through a range of distinct symptoms that can profoundly affect interpersonal relationships and emotional well-being. Individuals with NPD often exhibit an inflated sense of self-importance, which can lead to a constant need for admiration and validation from others. They may present themselves as superior, expecting special treatment and displaying a lack of empathy for those around them. This self-centered behavior often alienates family members and friends, leaving them feeling undervalued and emotionally drained. The struggle for those in close proximity to a narcissist is not only understanding the disorder but also recognizing the damage it inflicts on their own mental health.

Diagnosis of NPD is typically performed by a mental health professional through careful assessment and observation. Clinicians utilize the Diagnostic and Statistical Manual of Mental Disorders (DSM-5) criteria, which includes specific behavioral patterns such as grandiosity, preoccupation with success and power, and an inability to recognize or care for the feelings of others. Furthermore, individuals with NPD often have unstable relationships characterized by a cycle of idealization and devaluation. This diagnostic process is crucial because it helps differentiate between narcissistic traits, which many may exhibit, and the full-blown disorder that requires intervention.

The emotional toll of interacting with a narcissist can be overwhelming for victims of narcissistic abuse. They often find themselves questioning their worth and feeling trapped in a cycle of manipulation and emotional neglect. Symptoms of trauma can emerge, including anxiety, depression, and a pervasive sense of confusion about the nature of their relationship. Understanding the symptoms of NPD not only fosters awareness but also empowers those affected to recognize their own feelings and validate their experiences. By identifying these patterns, survivors can begin to reclaim their sense of self and establish healthier boundaries.

In the journey toward healing, it is essential to foster emotional intelligence, which serves as a protective shield against the toxic influence of narcissism. Developing skills such as self-awareness, self-regulation, and empathy can equip individuals with the tools necessary to navigate relationships more effectively. This growth can lead to improved decision-making, stronger relationships, and enhanced resilience in the face of emotional turmoil. By prioritizing personal development, survivors can break free from the patterns of abuse and cultivate healthier interactions that honor their emotional needs.

Ultimately, the path to recovery from narcissistic abuse involves not only understanding the symptoms and diagnosis of NPD but also integrating strategies for emotional management and personal growth. Building a support system, seeking therapy, and engaging in self-care practices are vital steps in the healing process. By raising awareness about the impact of narcissism and equipping oneself with knowledge, individuals can empower themselves and others, paving the way for healthier relationships and a brighter emotional future. The journey may be challenging, but with perseverance and support, it is possible to move beyond the shadows of narcissistic influence and embrace a life of authenticity and connection.

The Role of Empathy

Empathy serves as a crucial counterbalance to the traits commonly associated with narcissism. In understanding the narcissist's spectrum, recognizing the importance of empathy helps illuminate the emotional landscape that separates the narcissistic individual from those who can form genuine connections. Empathy allows individuals to step outside their own experiences to understand and share the feelings of others. This capacity for emotional resonance fosters healthier relationships and a deeper understanding of human experience, which starkly contrasts the self-centeredness often seen in narcissistic behavior.

In the realm of romantic relationships, empathy can be a transformative force. When one partner demonstrates empathy, it opens the door to vulnerability and connection, creating a safe space for both individuals to express their thoughts and emotions. Conversely, a lack of empathy in a relationship dominated by narcissistic traits can lead to manipulation and emotional turmoil. By recognizing the disparity in empathetic engagement, individuals can better discern whether they are in a relationship that uplifts them or one that drains their emotional well-being. Understanding this dynamic is essential for anyone hoping to navigate the complexities of love while preserving their self-worth.

Workplace environments are similarly influenced by the presence or absence of empathy. In teams where empathy flourishes, collaboration and innovation thrive. Employees feel valued and understood, fostering a culture of mutual respect. However, in workplaces overshadowed by narcissism, empathy is often replaced with competition and self-interest. This can lead to toxic work cultures where emotional manipulation and power struggles are commonplace. Recognizing these dynamics empowers individuals to seek healthier work environments or advocate for change within their organizations, promoting a culture that celebrates empathy and emotional intelligence.

Having a narcissistic parent can be particularly challenging, as the absence of empathy can profoundly affect familial dynamics. Children raised in such environments often struggle to develop their own empathetic skills, leading to a cycle of emotional detachment. However, understanding this cycle offers an opportunity for healing. By fostering empathy in oneself and others, individuals can break free from the patterns established by narcissistic parenting. Engaging in conversations about feelings, modeling empathetic behavior, and encouraging open communication can cultivate a more nurturing atmosphere, paving the way for healthier emotional development.

Ultimately, the recognition and cultivation of empathy is a powerful tool in the journey toward healing from narcissistic relationships. It allows individuals to process their experiences, understand their emotional pain, and reclaim their sense of self. Additionally, empathy serves as a foundation for establishing boundaries and identifying narcissistic traits in others, whether in friendships or romantic entanglements. As one learns to embrace empathy, the path toward recovery becomes clearer, facilitating a deeper understanding of both oneself and the nuances of human relationships.

FROM BLISS TO BETRAYAL: Navigating Relationships with Narcissists from Idealization to Discard

UNDERSTANDING NARCISSISTIC ABUSE

The Nature of Narcissism

As I mentioned before, Narcissism, at its core, manifests as an inflated sense of self-importance, a deep need for excessive admiration, and a profound lack of empathy for others. This personality trait can create a toxic environment for those caught in its orbit, often leading to emotional exhaustion and psychological trauma. Individuals entangled in relationships with narcissists frequently experience a shift in their self-worth and identity, often becoming mere reflections of their partner's distorted self-image. Understanding the nature of narcissism is crucial for those seeking to heal from the chaos it inflicts, as it lays the groundwork for recognizing the patterns of abuse and reclaiming one's sense of self.

The emotional toll of narcissistic relationships can lead to the formation of trauma bonds, a connection that is often characterized by cycles of idealization and devaluation. Victims may find themselves oscillating between moments of affection and emotional withdrawal, creating a powerful, albeit toxic, attachment. This cycle can be debilitating, leading to a sense of helplessness and confusion. Acknowledging the existence of trauma bonds is essential for breaking free from these destructive relationships, as it allows individuals to identify the manipulative dynamics at play and begin the process of disentangling themselves from the emotional chaos.

The aftermath of a relationship with a narcissist can be profound, often resulting in symptoms akin to post-traumatic stress disorder (PTSD). Victims may grapple with flashbacks, heightened anxiety, and depressive episodes as they navigate their healing journey. It is vital to understand that PTSD is not merely a disorder; it is an injury that requires compassion and care. This perspective empowers survivors to seek appropriate treatment and support, fostering a mindset that prioritizes healing over stigmatization. By recognizing PTSD as an injury, individuals can take proactive steps toward recovery, emphasizing the importance of self-care and professional guidance.

Post-traumatic growth is a possible outcome for those who have endured narcissistic abuse. While the journey may be fraught with challenges, it can also lead to newfound strength and resilience. Survivors often emerge from these experiences with a deeper understanding of themselves and their needs, paving the way for healthier relationships in the future. Embracing this growth mindset involves reframing trauma as a catalyst for transformation, allowing individuals to reclaim their narratives and redefine their futures. It is through this lens that survivors can cultivate a sense of agency and purpose, empowering them to thrive in the aftermath of their experiences.

Finally, coping mechanisms play a crucial role in managing the symptoms resulting from narcissistic abuse. Developing strategies for emotional regulation, engaging in therapy, and building a supportive community can significantly aid in the healing process. It is essential for survivors to seek validation and understanding from trusted sources while also learning to identify and overcome suicidal ideation that may arise from their trauma. By equipping themselves with effective coping skills and surrounding themselves with positive influences, survivors can navigate their path to recovery with hope and determination, ultimately redefining their relationship with themselves and the world around them.

Emotional Drainage: Recognizing the Signs

Emotional drainage is a subtle yet profound experience, often creeping in unnoticed until it becomes overwhelming. For those recovering from narcissistic abuse, the signs can manifest in various ways, deeply intertwined with the trauma bonds formed during the relationship. Recognizing these signs is the first step towards reclaiming one's emotional energy and well-being. Individuals may find themselves feeling persistently fatigued, not just physically but emotionally drained as well. This fatigue can stem from the relentless need to navigate the emotional landscapes created by a narcissist, where their needs and desires overshadow your own.

Disconnection from one's own feelings and desires. After prolonged exposure to a narcissistic partner, many adults begin to feel numb or apathetic, unable to identify what truly brings them joy or fulfillment. This emotional detachment is a defense mechanism, a way to cope with the chaos and manipulation that they have endured. It is crucial to understand this disconnection as a signal of the damage inflicted by the relationship, rather than a personal failure. Acknowledging this can pave the way for healing, allowing individuals to reconnect with their emotions and start to rediscover themselves.

Sleep disturbances often accompany emotional drainage, manifesting as insomnia or restless nights filled with anxiety. The mind races with thoughts of self-doubt, fear, and unresolved trauma, making it difficult to find peace. These disturbances can exacerbate feelings of depression and anxiety, creating a vicious cycle that further drains emotional resources. Understanding that these symptoms are linked to past experiences rather than personal inadequacies can empower individuals to seek the help they need, whether through therapy, support groups, or self-care practices that promote restorative sleep and relaxation.

Social withdrawal is another significant sign of emotional drainage. Many individuals recovering from narcissistic relationships may find themselves isolating from friends and family, feeling unworthy of connection or fearing judgment. This isolation can deepen feelings of loneliness and despair, further complicating the journey of healing. Recognizing the importance of community and support is vital in breaking this cycle of withdrawal. Reaching out, even when it feels challenging, can provide the encouragement needed to reintegrate into social circles and foster meaningful connections that promote healing.

Finally, the recognition of emotional drainage often leads to a critical turning point in the healing journey. By identifying these signs, individuals can begin to treat their PTSD as an injury in need of care rather than a disorder to be ashamed of. This shift in perception empowers survivors to prioritize their recovery, seek appropriate treatment, and cultivate coping mechanisms that nurture their emotional health. The journey towards post-traumatic growth is not linear, but by acknowledging the signs of emotional drainage, individuals can take the necessary steps to thrive after the chaos of narcissistic abuse, ultimately reclaiming their lives and their sense of self.

The Cycle of Abuse: Understanding the Patterns

The cycle of abuse is a pervasive pattern that often ensnares individuals in toxic relationships, creating a profound impact on their emotional well-being. Understanding this cycle is crucial for anyone seeking to break free from the grips of a narcissistic partner. The cycle typically includes phases of idealization, devaluation, and discard, each contributing to the emotional turmoil that victims endure. Recognizing these phases empowers individuals to identify harmful behaviors and take proactive steps toward healing and recovery.

In the idealization phase, the narcissist showers their partner with affection and attention, creating a façade of a perfect relationship. This initial intensity can be intoxicating, leading the victim to feel deeply valued and loved. The journey often begins with idealization, where the narcissist showers their partner with excessive praise and attention, creating an illusion of a perfect relationship.

This phase is marked by love bombing, where the narcissist's charm and adoration make the victim feel uniquely special. The psychological impact of this stage can be profound, as it fosters an intense emotional connection that can lead the victim to overlook potential red flags. Victims may find themselves entranced by the attention and affection, believing they have found a soulmate.

However, this phase is often short-lived, as the narcissist's insecurities and need for control soon manifest through manipulation and criticism.

Understanding the Idealization Phase in Narcissistic Relationships

Signs of Idealization

The idealization phase in relationships with narcissists is characterized by intense admiration and affection directed toward the partner. During this stage, the narcissist often shower their target with compliments, attention, and affection, creating an illusion of a perfect relationship. This behavior is often referred to as love bombing, where the narcissist employs flattery and grand gestures to captivate their victim.

The recipient of this admiration may feel special and desired, leading to a strong emotional connection that can cloud their judgment about the relationship's dynamics.

It is crucial to recognize that this overwhelming affection can be a manipulation tactic rather than genuine love.

Narcissists often portray an exaggerated version of themselves during the idealization phase. They might share grandiose stories about their achievements, skills, or social status to establish a sense of superiority. This self-promotion can create a sense of awe in their partner, further deepening the emotional bond. The partner, caught in this web of admiration, may ignore any red flags or inconsistencies in the narcissist's behavior. This stage is designed to foster dependency, making the victim more susceptible to the inevitable devaluation that follows.

Another significant sign of idealization is the narcissist's tendency to mirror their partner's interests, values, and desires. This strategic mimicry can create a false sense of compatibility, making the partner feel understood and valued. However, this mirroring is often superficial and serves to enhance the narcissist's control over the relationship. As the partner becomes enamored with the perceived similarities, they may overlook the lack of authenticity in the narcissist's character. This dynamic sets the stage for the manipulation and emotional turmoil that will ensue once the idealization phase comes to an end.

Idealization can lead to a distorted perception of the relationship, where the partner may believe they have found their soulmate. This phenomenon is often exacerbated by gaslighting, where the narcissist subtly undermines the partner's reality, causing confusion and self-doubt. The victim may begin to question their feelings, believing that any discomfort arises from their shortcomings rather than the narcissist's behavior. This psychological manipulation reinforces the partner's dependence on the narcissist, making it even more challenging to recognize the unhealthy dynamics at play.

Understanding the signs of idealization is essential for individuals navigating relationships with narcissists. Awareness of this phase can empower victims to identify the early warning signs of emotional manipulation and control. Recognizing that idealization is often a precursor to devaluation can help partners maintain a more objective view of the relationship. By fostering self-awareness and establishing boundaries, individuals can protect themselves from the cyclical nature of narcissistic abuse and begin to reclaim their sense of self outside the confines of the toxic relationship.

The allure of idealization in narcissistic relationships captivates many, drawing them into a web of charm and affection that often feels like a dream come true. During this initial phase, the narcissist projects an image of perfection, showering their target with attention, compliments, and affection. This intense focus creates an illusion of a deep connection, leading the victim to feel uniquely valued and adored. The narcissist's ability to mirror the desires and needs of their partner fosters an intoxicating bond, often blinding individuals to the underlying manipulative dynamics at play. This phase, often characterized by love bombing, can feel exhilarating, as the recipient of such affection believes they have found their ideal partner.

As the relationship progresses, the dynamics begin to shift, revealing the darker aspects of this idealization phase. While the initial charm can feel enchanting, it is essential to recognize that it is often a façade designed to ensnare the victim. The narcissist employs gaslighting techniques during this stage, subtly manipulating the perceptions of their partner to maintain control.

By distorting reality, the narcissist ensures that their target remains enthralled by the illusion they have created, often leading to dependency and a profound sense of attachment. This psychological manipulation can leave the victim questioning their self-worth, as they begin to internalize the false narrative constructed by the narcissist.

The Role of Gaslighting During the Idealization Stage

What is Gaslighting?

Gaslighting is a psychological manipulation tactic often employed by narcissists to gain control over their partners. It involves making someone doubt their own perceptions, memories, or understanding of events. This insidious form of emotional abuse can lead victims to feel confused, anxious, and insecure about their reality. In the context of narcissistic relationships, gaslighting typically occurs during the idealization phase, where the narcissist initially portrays themselves as the perfect partner. The charming facade can quickly dissolve as the relationship shifts, leaving the partner questioning their own sanity.

Recognizing gaslighting as a significant component of the narcissistic relationship cycle is essential for recovery. By understanding its role, victims can begin to reclaim their sense of reality and self-worth. Recovery strategies may include therapy, support groups, and educational resources that empower individuals to trust their own perceptions once again. Acknowledging the effects of gaslighting is the first step toward healing, allowing survivors to break free from the cycle of manipulation and foster healthier relationships in the future.

Gaslighting during the idealization phase involves the narcissist subtly altering the victim's perception of reality. They may distort facts or minimize the victim's feelings, leading the victim to question their own thoughts and emotions. For instance, a narcissist might claim that the victim is overly sensitive when they express discomfort about certain behaviors. This manipulation creates confusion and self-doubt, making the victim more reliant on the narcissist for validation. The idealization stage, therefore, is not merely about affection; it is a calculated strategy to establish control while simultaneously presenting a facade of love and support.

Recognizing the signs of gaslighting during the idealization phase is crucial for victims. These signs may include an increase in compliments followed by sudden shifts to criticism, or the narcissist's insistence that they know what is best for the victim. Victims may find themselves feeling increasingly insecure, as their perceptions of what is normal in a relationship become distorted. Understanding these patterns can empower individuals to identify when they are being manipulated and to take steps to protect their mental health.

Recovery from the impact of gaslighting and the subsequent devaluation requires a deliberate process of reclaiming one's sense of self.

Love Bombing: The Initial Charm of Narcissistic Partners

Love bombing, a tactic often employed during the idealization phase, serves as a critical warning sign of potential narcissistic behavior. The overwhelming affection can create a false sense of security, making it difficult for victims to recognize the eventual devaluation and discard. This manipulation can leave deep psychological scars, as victims may equate the initial love with genuine care, only to find it was a façade. Understanding love bombing can empower individuals to establish boundaries and maintain a healthier perspective on relationships.

Characteristics of Love Bombing

Love bombing is a manipulative tactic commonly employed by narcissists during the initial stages of a relationship, serving as a powerful tool for idealization. This phase is characterized by an overwhelming display of affection, attention, and admiration that can be intoxicating for the recipient. Narcissists often shower their partners with compliments, gifts, and grand gestures, creating an illusion of a perfect relationship. This excessive adoration is designed to foster a deep emotional connection quickly, making the target feel special and valued, while simultaneously establishing control over them.

One of the defining characteristics of love bombing is its intensity. The attention and affection are not only abundant but also disproportionate to the length of the relationship. This rapid escalation often leaves the recipient feeling as though they have found their soulmate or a once-in-a-lifetime connection. Narcissists thrive on this whirlwind dynamic, as it allows them to manipulate their partner's emotions and foster dependency. The partner may begin to overlook red flags or inconsistencies in the narcissist's behavior, blinded by the initial charm and excitement.

Another significant characteristic of love bombing is its inconsistency. While the initial period is filled with affection and adoration, it is often followed by a stark contrast during the devaluation phase. Once the narcissist feels they have secured their partner's attachment, the same behaviors that once felt so genuine may turn cold and dismissive. This inconsistency can create confusion and emotional turmoil for the partner, who struggles to reconcile the loving gestures with the subsequent neglect or criticism that follows. Such erratic behavior reinforces the control the narcissist has over their partner's emotional state.

Additionally, love bombing can create an environment of dependency. The intense focus and validation provided by the narcissist can lead the partner to develop a heightened sense of self-worth that is contingent upon the narcissist's approval. This dependency is strategic, as it keeps the partner invested in the relationship despite the emerging signs of manipulation. Over time, the recipient may find themselves craving the affection they once received, making them more susceptible to future emotional abuse and manipulation.

Lastly, love bombing can have lasting psychological effects on the victim, even after the relationship has ended. The initial euphoria can create a sense of longing and nostalgia for the idealized moments, making it difficult for the victim to move on. This emotional turmoil can lead to self-doubt and confusion about one's worth, as the victim grapples with the stark contrast between the intense love bombing and the subsequent devaluation. Recognizing love bombing as a tactic of manipulation is crucial for individuals navigating relationships with narcissists, as it empowers them to identify unhealthy patterns and reclaim their emotional autonomy.

The Psychological Effects on Victims

The psychological effects on victims of narcissistic relationships are profound and often long-lasting. In the idealization phase, victims experience intense emotional highs brought on by the narcissist's charm and affection. This love bombing creates a dependency, as the victim feels special and valued. However, this initial adoration is superficial, designed to manipulate and control. As the relationship progresses, the victim may struggle to reconcile the early bliss with the subsequent emotional turmoil, leading to confusion and cognitive dissonance about their partner's true nature.

As the relationship shifts into devaluation, victims may encounter a stark contrast to the idealization phase. The narcissist employs critical remarks, belittlement, and emotional withdrawal, which can devastate the victim's self-esteem. This devaluation phase is often marked by gaslighting, where the victim is made to question their reality and perceptions. Such manipulation can leave victims feeling isolated, anxious, and doubting their sense of self. The psychological impact of this phase can manifest as depression, anxiety, and a pervasive sense of worthlessness, making it difficult for victims to recognize the unhealthy dynamics at play.

Love bombing, a hallmark of the early stages of the relationship, serves as a powerful tool for narcissists to ensnare their victims. This initial charm creates a false sense of security, leading victims to believe they have found their ideal partner. However, once the narcissist feels they have exerted enough control, the love bombing is replaced with manipulation and emotional abuse. Victims often find themselves reflecting on the initial affection, creating a painful longing for the moments of connection that now feel unattainable. This longing can hinder recovery and complicate the healing process.

The silent treatment is the ultimate tool that narcissists frequently use to exert control and manipulate their partners. This tactic creates an atmosphere of tension and uncertainty, making victims feel anxious and desperate for validation. It can serve as a punishment for perceived slights or as a way to regain control after the narcissist feels threatened. Learning to cope with the silent treatment and recognizing it as a form of emotional abuse is vital for recovery. By understanding each stage of the narcissistic cycle, individuals can develop effective recovery strategies and regain their sense of self-worth.

The transition into the devaluation phase marks a stark contrast, where the once-beloved partner becomes the target of blame and emotional abuse, leaving the victim feeling confused and unworthy. As the relationship progresses, the dynamics shift into devaluation. Here, the initial charm begins to fade, revealing the narcissist's true nature. The once adoring partner may become critical, dismissive, and emotionally abusive. Victims often experience confusion and self-doubt as the narcissist employs tactics such as gaslighting to undermine their reality.

This stage is psychologically damaging, as it erodes the victim's self-esteem and sense of worth. Recognizing the signs of devaluation is essential for victims to understand that the love they initially received may have been conditional and manipulative.

The Psychological Impact of Devaluation by Narcissists

Recognizing Devaluation

Recognizing devaluation in relationships with narcissists is crucial for understanding the dynamics at play and protecting oneself from emotional harm. Devaluation often follows the idealization phase, where the narcissist initially showers their partner with affection and admiration. This phase can create a false sense of security that masks the impending emotional turmoil. As the relationship progresses, the idealized partner is gradually subjected to criticism, belittlement, and emotional withdrawal, signaling the beginning of devaluation. This shift can be subtle at first, with the narcissist employing tactics designed to undermine the partner's self-esteem while maintaining a facade of care.

The psychological impact of devaluation is profound and can lead to significant emotional distress for the victim. As the narcissist begins to diminish their partner's worth, the victim may experience confusion, self-doubt, and a loss of identity. Gaslighting often accompanies this phase, as the narcissist manipulates reality, making the victim question their perceptions and feelings. The once-loving partner's belittling remarks and dismissive attitudes create a toxic environment where the victim feels trapped, unsure of themselves, and increasingly reliant on the narcissist for validation. Recognizing these signs is essential for victims to reclaim their sense of self and begin the healing process.

Identifying the signs of discard is also critical in the context of devaluation. The discard phase often manifests when the narcissist has extracted all the emotional fuel they desire, leading them to seek new sources of validation. This can result in sudden emotional detachment, withdrawal of affection, and an abrupt end to communication. Victims may find themselves grappling with feelings of abandonment and betrayal, as the relationship they once cherished disintegrates before their eyes. Understanding that this behavior is a hallmark of narcissistic relationships can help victims process their emotions and prepare for the challenges that lie ahead.

Love bombing, the excessive affection and attention given by the narcissist during the initial stages of the relationship, plays a significant role in setting the stage for devaluation. This intense period of charm can create an illusion of a perfect relationship, making the eventual shift to devaluation all the more shocking. Victims may find it hard to reconcile the loving words and actions from the beginning with the current reality of criticism and neglect. Recognizing this cycle is essential for victims to break free from the emotional rollercoaster and to understand that the initial affection was a strategy rather than genuine love.

The silent treatment is another common tool employed by narcissists to exert control during the devaluation phase. This method of emotional manipulation can leave victims feeling isolated and desperate for resolution. The absence of communication not only punishes the victim but also reinforces the narcissist's power in the relationship. Understanding the silent treatment as a control mechanism allows victims to see the situation clearly, enabling them to detach emotionally and seek support. By recognizing these patterns, individuals can better navigate the tumultuous landscape of relationships with narcissists and ultimately reclaim their autonomy and self-worth.

The discard phase... As the cycle continues, the discard phase often follows, resulting in a devastating emotional fallout for the victim. The narcissist may abruptly cut ties or continue to engage in intermittent reinforcement, withdrawing affection only to reintroduce it sporadically. This inconsistency keeps the victim trapped in a state of longing and despair, often resulting in a cycle of hope and disappointment. Understanding this cycle allows victims to see the relationship for what it truly is—a destructive pattern designed to maintain the narcissist's control at the expense of the victim's emotional health

The discard phase can also be gradual, leaving victims feeling abandoned and betrayed. The narcissist typically deems their partner no longer useful or entertaining, leading to a cold withdrawal of affection. This stage can manifest in various ways, from outright termination of the relationship to a more insidious emotional distancing. Victims may struggle with feelings of unworthiness and loss, questioning what went wrong and why they were cast aside. Acknowledging the discard as part of the narcissistic cycle can help victims process their experience and begin to heal.

The discard phase can be particularly traumatic for victims, as it often involves a sudden severing of the relationship. Victims may be left struggling to comprehend the abrupt end to what initially seemed like a passionate connection. This phase is marked by a sense of loss and grief, as victims grapple with the emotional fallout of being discarded. The narcissist's lack of empathy during this phase compounds the pain, as they may move on to another relationship quickly, leaving the victim feeling discarded and unworthy.

Recognizing the Signs of Discard in Narcissistic Abuse

Indicators of Discard

Indicators of Discard often manifest subtly at first, but they can escalate and become increasingly apparent as the relationship with a narcissist progresses. One of the most telling signs is a sudden decrease in communication. Initially, the narcissist may have bombarded their partner with messages and attention, creating an illusion of deep connection. However, as the discard phase approaches, this communication can dwindle significantly. The partner may find themselves reaching out more often, only to receive sparse or curt responses. This shift can leave the victim feeling confused and anxious, questioning what went wrong in the relationship.

CRITICISM AND CONTEMPT Another indicator is the emergence of criticism and contempt. During the idealization phase, the narcissist typically showers their partner with praise and admiration. However, as they begin to devalue their partner, the tone shifts dramatically. Disparaging comments, subtle jabs, or overt hostility may begin to surface, often disguised as jokes or casual remarks. This devaluation serves a dual purpose: it bolsters the narcissist's self-esteem and sets the stage for the discard. Victims may find themselves walking on eggshells, trying to avoid triggering further criticism while grappling with their dwindling self-worth.

ISOLATION is another critical indicator of impending discard. Narcissists often work to separate their partners from friends and family, creating a dependency that makes it difficult for the victim to leave. As the discard phase nears, they may intensify this isolation, either by sabotaging social engagements or by planting seeds of doubt about the partner's relationships. The victim may become increasingly reliant on the narcissist, which can lead to feelings of helplessness. This isolation not only prevents the victim from seeking support but also reinforces the narcissist's control over the relationship.

GASLIGHTING is also prevalent during this phase. The narcissist may distort reality to make the victim question their perceptions and memories, thereby diminishing their sense of self. This tactic can be particularly disorienting, as it leads the victim to doubt their own experiences and feelings. As the narcissist prepares for discard, they may escalate their gaslighting behaviors, making the victim feel increasingly unstable. This psychological manipulation can leave lasting scars, complicating the victim's recovery process once the relationship ends.

A DISTINCT LACK OF EMPATHY emerges as a clear sign of discard. Narcissists often demonstrate a pronounced inability to empathize with their partners, particularly as they prepare to exit the relationship. During the discard phase, this lack of empathy becomes stark; the narcissist may exhibit indifference to their partner's emotional pain or distress. Victims may find themselves expressing their feelings only to be met with coldness or dismissal. This emotional detachment can be profoundly hurtful, underscoring the finality of the relationship and reinforcing the pain of the discard. Recognizing these indicators is crucial for victims, as it can empower them to seek support and begin the journey toward healing.

Emotional Repercussions of Being Discarded

The emotional repercussions of being discarded by a narcissist can be profound and long-lasting. After experiencing the initial idealization phase, where the narcissist showers their partner with affection and attention, the sudden shift to devaluation and discard can leave the victim feeling bewildered and abandoned. This abrupt change can evoke feelings of worthlessness, confusion, and intense grief, as the victim grapples with the loss of the idealized relationship they once believed in. The emotional turmoil often stems from the stark contrast between the love bombing phase and the coldness of the discard, creating a psychological fracture that is difficult to mend.

RANGE OF EMOTIONS Victims of narcissistic discard frequently experience a range of emotions, including betrayal, anger, and sadness. The sense of betrayal is particularly acute, as the victim may have invested significant emotional energy into the relationship, only to have that investment disregarded. Those feelings can be compounded by the narcissist's tendency to gaslight their partner, leading them to question their reality and perceptions. This can create a toxic cycle where the victim feels responsible for the relationship's failure, further deepening their emotional pain and complicating their healing process.

THE SILENT TREATMENT is another weapon in the narcissist's arsenal that can exacerbate the emotional fallout from being discarded. By withdrawing communication and affection, the narcissist reinforces feelings of isolation and abandonment. Victims may struggle with self-doubt, wondering if they did something wrong to deserve such treatment. This tactic not only serves to control the victim but also heightens their emotional distress, making the process of recovery more challenging. The lack of closure often leaves victims haunted by unanswered questions, which can impede their ability to move forward.

Recovery strategies after experiencing narcissistic devaluation and discard are crucial for regaining a sense of self-worth and emotional stability.

1. Victims must first acknowledge the reality of their experiences, understanding that the narcissist's behavior is a reflection of their own issues rather than a commentary on the victim's value.
2. Establishing a support network of friends, family, or therapists who understand the dynamics of narcissistic relationships can provide a safe space for healing.
3. Engaging in self-care practices and setting boundaries are also essential steps in reclaiming one's identity and emotional well-being.

Ultimately, navigating the emotional repercussions of being discarded by a narcissist involves a journey toward self-discovery and healing. Recognizing the signs of discard and understanding the psychological impact of the preceding stages—idealization, devaluation, and love bombing—can empower victims to break free from the cycle of narcissistic abuse. By fostering self-compassion and resilience, individuals can learn to rebuild their lives and develop healthier, more fulfilling relationships in the future.

The Ultimate Tool for Control in Narcissistic Dynamics

Understanding the Silent Treatment

The silent treatment is a common and insidious tactic employed by narcissists during their relationships. It serves as a form of emotional manipulation, leaving the victim in a state of confusion and emotional distress. By withdrawing communication and affection, the narcissist exerts control over their partner, creating a power imbalance that reinforces their dominance. This behavior often emerges during the devaluation phase when the narcissist feels threatened or dissatisfied. The silence is not merely a lack of communication; it is a calculated strategy to elicit feelings of guilt and inadequacy in the victim.

The impact of the silent treatment on the victim can be profound. It can lead to feelings of isolation, anxiety, and self-doubt. As the narcissist withdraws, the victim may internalize the silence as a reflection of their worth, questioning what they did wrong to provoke such treatment. This emotional turmoil can trigger a cycle of seeking validation from the narcissist, reinforcing their control and perpetuating the dysfunctional dynamic. Victims may find themselves walking on eggshells, constantly trying to decipher the reasons behind the narcissist's withdrawal and striving to regain their affection.

In the context of narcissistic relationships, the silent treatment can also serve as a form of punishment. When the narcissist feels that their partner has crossed a boundary or failed to meet their expectations, they may resort to this tactic to assert their power. This punishment is not always explicit; instead, it manifests as a chilling silence that speaks volumes. The victim, desperate for connection, may go to great lengths to appease the narcissist, often compromising their own needs and desires in the process. This dynamic fosters a toxic environment where the victim's emotional health deteriorates over time.

Recognizing the silent treatment as a form of emotional abuse is crucial for those navigating relationships with narcissists. Understanding that this behavior is not a reflection of personal failure but rather a strategic maneuver by the narcissist can empower victims to break free from the cycle of manipulation. It is essential to set boundaries and seek support from trusted friends or mental health professionals who can provide guidance and validation. Acknowledging the impact of the silent treatment is a vital step in reclaiming one's sense of self and breaking the hold of the narcissist's control.

Ultimately, healing from the effects of the silent treatment requires a commitment to self-care and self-compassion. Victims must prioritize their emotional well-being, recognizing that they are deserving of healthy communication and respect in their relationships. Engaging in therapy, practicing mindfulness, and fostering supportive connections can aid in recovery. By understanding the nature of the silent treatment and its role in the cycle of narcissistic abuse, individuals can begin to reclaim their voice and navigate their path toward healing and empowerment.

The Effects on Victim's Mental Health

The effects of narcissistic relationships on a victim's mental health can be profound and long-lasting. The idealization phase, where the narcissist showers the victim with love and attention, can create an intoxicating experience that leads the victim to feel valued and special. However, this initial charm often masks underlying manipulation. Victims may become emotionally dependent on the idealized version of their partner, leading to an unhealthy attachment that clouds their judgment. This dependence can set the stage for subsequent phases of the relationship, where the impact on mental health begins to degrade significantly.

As the relationship transitions into the devaluation phase, the victim often experiences a sharp decline in self-esteem and confidence. The narcissist's criticisms and emotional withdrawal can create a pervasive sense of inadequacy in the victim. This devaluation is not just a temporary setback; it can create lasting psychological scars. Victims frequently internalize the negative messages from their partners, leading to anxiety, depression, and a distorted self-image. The psychological impact of being belittled and dismissed can result in a deep-seated sense of worthlessness, making it challenging for victims to reclaim their identity after the relationship ends.

The discard phase is particularly devastating for victims. After experiencing the highs of idealization and the lows of devaluation, being discarded can feel like an emotional death. The abruptness of this phase can leave victims in a state of shock and confusion, often spiraling into depression and isolation. The sudden loss of what they believed was a meaningful relationship can lead to intense feelings of abandonment and betrayal. Additionally, the way a narcissist often exits — sometimes with no explanation — can amplify feelings of rejection, further exacerbating the victim's mental health struggles.

Coping mechanisms play a crucial role in recovery after experiencing narcissistic abuse. Victims may initially struggle to understand what they've gone through, often needing time to process their experiences. Engaging in therapy can provide essential support, helping victims rebuild their self-esteem and develop healthier coping strategies. Support groups can also be beneficial, as they offer a sense of community and validation. Learning to recognize the signs of love bombing and the silent treatment can empower victims to set boundaries in future relationships, fostering resilience and self-awareness.

Navigating the aftermath of a relationship with a narcissist requires a multifaceted approach to healing. Victims must confront the psychological aftermath of each stage, from idealization to discard, to fully understand the impact on their mental health. By acknowledging their experiences and seeking appropriate support, victims can gradually reclaim their sense of self and work towards healthier, more fulfilling relationships in the future. Awareness of the cyclical nature of narcissistic abuse can also equip individuals with the knowledge to break free from toxic patterns, promoting long-term emotional well-being.

The Impact of the Abuse Cycle on Victims

The cycle of narcissistic abuse is a complex web that significantly impacts victims at each stage: idealization, devaluation, and discard. During the idealization phase, victims often experience intense affection and admiration, known as love bombing. This stage can create a euphoric sense of connection, leading victims to feel cherished and valued. However, this initial charm can be deceptive, as it sets the groundwork for the unpredictable shifts that follow. Victims may find themselves entrapped in a relationship that promises fulfillment but ultimately leads to emotional turmoil.

As the relationship progresses into the devaluation phase, the initial admiration is replaced by criticism, manipulation, and emotional neglect. Narcissists use various tactics, including gaslighting, to undermine their partner's self-esteem and sense of reality. Victims may struggle to recognize the shift, often blaming themselves for the changes in their partner's behavior. The psychological impact of this devaluation can be profound, leading to anxiety, depression, and a pervasive sense of worthlessness. Victims may become isolated, feeling trapped in a cycle of self-doubt and confusion as they attempt to navigate their partner's erratic emotional landscape.

When the relationship reaches the discard stage, victims often face a painful and abrupt end to the connection they once cherished. This stage can be marked by the silent treatment, where the narcissist withdraws and refuses to communicate, leaving victims feeling abandoned and rejected. The emotional fallout from being discarded can be devastating, as individuals grapple with feelings of betrayal and loss. Many victims may find it challenging to understand what went wrong, as they reflect on the idealization that initially drew them in. This lack of closure can exacerbate feelings of confusion and grief.

The Impact on Mental Health

The impact of narcissistic abuse on mental health is profound and often underestimated. Victims frequently experience a range of psychological issues, including PTSD, depression, and anxiety, which can stem from the emotional turmoil that accompanies such toxic relationships. The relentless manipulation, gaslighting, and emotional draining leave deep scars, making it essential to recognize that these are not merely disorders but injuries in need of care. Understanding this distinction can empower individuals to seek appropriate treatment and support, enabling them to reclaim their lives.

Recovery Strategies After Experiencing Narcissistic Devaluation

Healing from Devaluation

Healing from devaluation in relationships with narcissists is a complex process that requires time, self-reflection, and support. The devaluation phase often follows the initial idealization, where the partner's worth seems to diminish drastically. This shift can be jarring and leave lasting emotional scars. Understanding that devaluation is a tactic used by narcissists to gain control can help victims begin to detach their self-worth from the opinions and behaviors of their abuser. Knowing that the devaluation is a reflection of the narcissist's issues, rather than one's personal deficiencies, is a crucial step toward healing.

Recognizing the psychological impact of devaluation is essential. Victims often experience feelings of confusion, inadequacy, and self-doubt as they are subjected to constant criticism and manipulation. This phase can lead to internalized beliefs of worthlessness, prompting individuals to question their identity and value. Acknowledging these feelings is the first step in the recovery process. It's important to validate these experiences and understand that they are a normal response to the emotional turmoil inflicted by a narcissistic partner. Seeking professional help, such as therapy, can provide a safe space for individuals to process their experiences and rebuild their self-esteem.

Recovery strategies after experiencing narcissistic devaluation are varied and should be tailored to each individual's needs. Building a support network of friends, family, or support groups can offer encouragement and remind victims of their inherent worth. Engaging in self-care practices, such as mindfulness, journaling, or creative outlets, can aid in emotional processing and help individuals reconnect with their authentic selves. Additionally, educating oneself about narcissistic behavior and the dynamics of such relationships can empower victims, allowing them to recognize patterns and establish healthier boundaries in future relationships.

Coping mechanisms for victims of narcissistic discard are also vital in the healing process. It's common for individuals to experience a sense of loss and betrayal during this stage, as the abrupt end can leave them feeling abandoned. Developing coping strategies such as establishing routines, practicing gratitude, and focusing on personal goals can be beneficial. It is equally important to allow oneself to grieve the relationship and to process the emotions that arise. This acknowledgment of pain is a necessary part of moving forward, fostering resilience and a deeper understanding of one's needs and boundaries.

Healing from devaluation is a journey of rediscovering one's self-worth and resilience. It involves recognizing the patterns of narcissistic abuse and taking proactive steps toward recovery. By understanding the cycle of idealization, devaluation, and discard, individuals can break free from the toxic hold of narcissistic relationships. Embracing this journey not only facilitates personal growth but also lays the groundwork for healthier, more fulfilling relationships in the future. Each step taken toward healing is a testament to one's strength and a move toward reclaiming a life filled with authenticity and joy.

Rebuilding Self-Esteem

Rebuilding self-esteem after experiencing the tumultuous cycle of a relationship with a narcissist is a crucial step toward recovery and personal empowerment. The journey often begins with acknowledging the impact of the idealization phase, where the narcissist showers their partner with affection and attention, creating an illusion of a perfect relationship. During this phase, victims may feel validated and cherished, but as the relationship progresses, the narcissist shifts to devaluation, undermining their partner's self-worth. Recognizing this transition is vital for understanding how deeply ingrained feelings of inadequacy can develop, making the rebuilding process even more complex.

The devaluation stage is particularly damaging as it systematically erodes self-esteem. The narcissist may employ tactics such as criticism, belittling remarks, and emotional neglect. Victims often internalize these negative messages, leading them to question their value and capabilities. This psychological impact can linger long after the relationship has ended, manifesting as self-doubt and a diminished sense of self. It is essential for individuals to identify these feelings as products of the abusive dynamic rather than inherent flaws within themselves.

As victims transition to the discard phase, they may experience a profound sense of loss and confusion. The sudden removal of the narcissist's attention can leave individuals in a state of emotional turmoil. Recognizing the signs of discard, such as abrupt changes in communication or withdrawal of affection, helps victims understand that this behavior reflects the narcissist's patterns rather than their worth. Understanding this can be liberating and serves as a foundation for rebuilding self-esteem, allowing individuals to detach their self-worth from their former partner's actions.

Healing begins with the implementation of recovery strategies that focus on self-acceptance and self-compassion. Engaging in therapy or support groups can provide a safe space to process emotions and rebuild confidence. Establishing boundaries, practicing self-care, and cultivating new interests are effective ways to restore a sense of identity independent of the previous relationship. Additionally, developing a support network of friends and family who affirm one’s value can counteract the damaging messages received during the relationship.

Rebuilding self-esteem is an ongoing process that requires patience and perseverance. Victims must learn to challenge the negative beliefs instilled by the narcissist, replacing them with positive affirmations and self-recognition. This journey is not just about recovering from past pain but also about rediscovering one's strengths and abilities. By focusing on personal growth and resilience, individuals can emerge from the shadows of narcissistic relationships with a renewed sense of self-worth and the ability to engage in healthier relationships in the future.

Healing from such relationships necessitates a deep exploration of the self and the cultivation of emotional intelligence. Survivors must learn to recognize their worth outside of the narcissist's validation, fostering a sense of empowerment that comes from within. Techniques for recovery may include therapy, support groups, and self-reflection, all of which can help individuals rebuild their identity and establish healthier relationship patterns. By prioritizing emotional regulation, survivors can learn to manage trauma responses and navigate their healing journey with greater resilience and self-awareness. Recovery after experiencing narcissistic devaluation or discard requires a multifaceted approach. Victims must first recognize the manipulative tactics used against them, such as the silent treatment, which serves as a form of control and punishment. Developing coping mechanisms, seeking therapy, and establishing a support network are crucial steps in regaining a sense of self and autonomy. Understanding the cycle of narcissistic abuse, from idealization to discard, empowers victims to break free from the emotional chains that bind them and facilitates healing from the psychological scars left behind.

Raising awareness about the cycle of abuse is vital in promoting education and support for those affected by narcissistic relationships. By sharing knowledge about the signs and symptoms of narcissistic personality disorder, individuals can better equip themselves to identify red flags and protect their emotional health. Empowerment through education fosters a community of understanding, where victims can find solace and strength in their shared experiences. Breaking the cycle of abuse is not merely about survival; it is about thriving in a world where healthy, fulfilling relationships are possible.

THE TRAUMA BOND

The trauma bond created in relationships with narcissists can be particularly challenging. This bond often confuses feelings of love and attachment with the pain inflicted by the abuser. Victims may find themselves caught in a cycle of hope and despair, which can exacerbate mental health issues. Recognizing this bond as a tool of manipulation is the first step toward breaking free. By acknowledging the depth of this emotional entanglement, individuals can begin to confront the reality of their situation and take proactive steps towards healing.

What is a Trauma Bond?

A trauma bond is a complex emotional attachment that forms between an individual and their abuser, often rooted in a cycle of abuse interspersed with moments of affection or kindness. This bond can create a powerful sense of connection that makes it difficult for the victim to break free, even in the face of overwhelming pain. In the aftermath of a relationship with a narcissist, these bonds can perpetuate feelings of confusion, self-doubt, and despair. Understanding the nature of trauma bonds is essential for anyone seeking to reclaim their life after such a damaging experience.

The dynamics of a trauma bond often involve a pattern of manipulation and control, where the narcissist alternates between devaluation and idealization. Victims may find themselves clinging to the fleeting moments of love and validation, convinced that the abuser is the only one who can understand or fulfill them. This creates a distorted reality, where the pain of the relationship is overshadowed by the hope of reforming the connection. Recognizing this cycle is a critical step in the healing process, as it allows individuals to see the relationship for what it truly is rather than through the lens of emotional dependency.

Breaking free from a trauma bond requires immense courage and self-awareness. It involves acknowledging the hurt and betrayal while also confronting the internalized beliefs that the narcissist has instilled. Many victims struggle with feelings of guilt or shame, believing they are somehow responsible for the abuse they endured. This misconception can keep them tethered to their abuser, making recovery seem unattainable. By reframing PTSD as an injury rather than a disorder, individuals can begin to treat their emotional wounds with the same care and attention they would give to a physical injury, fostering a deeper understanding of their healing journey.

The path to healing from a trauma bond is not linear; it is filled with obstacles and setbacks. However, it is also an opportunity for post-traumatic growth. As individuals work through their pain, they can discover newfound strength, resilience, and clarity. This process may involve seeking professional support, engaging in self-care practices, and developing healthy coping mechanisms. Each step taken toward liberation from the trauma bond is a step toward empowerment and a chance to build a life free from the shadows of the past.

Ultimately, understanding trauma bonds is crucial for anyone recovering from narcissistic abuse. By recognizing the manipulative tactics employed by narcissists and the emotional turmoil they cause, individuals can begin to untangle themselves from these harmful connections. As they navigate their healing journey, they can redefine their relationship with themselves, cultivate healthier connections, and thrive in a future unburdened by the weight of trauma. Embracing this transformative process not only fosters personal growth but also inspires others who may be trapped in similar circumstances to seek their own freedom.

How Trauma Bonds Form

Trauma bonds typically form in relationships characterized by a cycle of abuse, wherein moments of intense emotional connection are interspersed with episodes of manipulation and control. This unique dynamic often leads individuals to develop a profound attachment to their abuser, despite the pain inflicted upon them. Such bonds can be misleading; the love and affection experienced during the highs can overshadow the deep emotional scars left by the lows. Understanding how these bonds form is crucial for anyone seeking to break free from the clutches of a narcissistic relationship and reclaim their sense of self.

At the heart of trauma bonding lies the unpredictability of the relationship. Victims often oscillate between euphoric love and devastating emotional turmoil. This rollercoaster creates a sense of dependency, where the victim feels compelled to please their abuser to avoid conflict and maintain the fleeting moments of affection. The intermittent reinforcement of kindness followed by cruelty reinforces a false sense of security, making it difficult for individuals to recognize the toxicity of their circumstances. The emotional highs become addictive, trapping victims in a cycle that can feel inescapable.

1. Additionally, the manipulation tactics employed by narcissists play a significant role in the formation of trauma bonds. Gaslighting, emotional blackmail, and other forms of psychological manipulation serve to erode the victim's self-esteem and sense of reality. This disorientation fosters a reliance

on the abuser for validation, creating an environment where the victim believes they cannot survive without the narcissist's approval or affection. Over time, this dependency morphs into a trauma bond, obscuring one's ability to see the relationship for what it truly is—a source of pain rather than love.

2. Recognizing the signs of trauma bonding is a critical step toward healing. Individuals may find themselves rationalizing the abuser's behavior or feeling guilt for wanting to leave the relationship. It is essential to confront these feelings and understand that they stem from a manipulated reality rather than genuine love. By reframing PTSD as an injury rather than a disorder, it becomes clear that healing is not only possible but necessary. Acknowledging the trauma bond allows individuals to start dismantling the negative beliefs that have been instilled in them, paving the way for recovery and growth.

3. Breaking free from trauma bonds is not an easy journey, but it is one filled with hope and potential for post-traumatic growth. With the right support, individuals can learn to redefine their identities outside of the relationship and reclaim their power. Therapy, self-care, and supportive communities can serve as vital resources in this transformative process. As victims begin to understand their worth and the falsehood of the bonds that held them captive, they can emerge stronger and more resilient, ready to embrace a future filled with healthier relationships and a renewed sense of self.

Post-traumatic growth is an inspiring concept that highlights the potential for personal transformation following adversity. While the journey through PTSD and the aftermath of narcissistic abuse is undeniably difficult, it can also lead to newfound strength and resilience. Individuals who have endured such experiences often emerge with a deeper understanding of their worth, enhanced empathy, and a renewed sense of purpose. Embracing this growth mindset can be a powerful catalyst for recovery, transforming pain into a source of empowerment.

SUICIDAL IDEATION

In addressing suicidal ideation that may arise from emotional abuse, it is crucial to foster open conversations about mental health. Many individuals feel isolated in their suffering, believing they are alone in their struggles. By creating supportive environments where people can share their experiences, we can dismantle the stigma surrounding mental health challenges. It is vital to encourage those affected by narcissistic abuse to seek help, whether through therapy, support groups, or community resources, reinforcing that they are not defined by their trauma but are capable of healing and thriving.

Ultimately, don't ignore the fact that redefining PTSD as an injury rather than a disorder shifts the narrative toward a more compassionate understanding of mental health. This perspective not only validates the experiences of survivors but also underscores the importance of comprehensive treatment approaches. Addressing PTSD with the seriousness it deserves allows for tailored interventions that meet the unique needs of those recovering from narcissistic abuse. With dedication and support, individuals can navigate their journey toward healing, reclaim their lives, and emerge stronger than before.

The narcissist seeks to control and diminish you, but you have the power to reclaim your narrative. Healing is about rewriting your story, a story of resilience, self-love, and authentic connection.

THE NATURE OF TOXIC RELATIONSHIPS

Description of Toxic Relationships

Toxic relationships often manifest in a cycle of manipulation, control, and emotional upheaval that leaves lasting scars on individuals. These relationships are characterized by an imbalance of power, where one partner seeks to dominate and belittle the other, often under the guise of love or concern. The toxic partner, frequently a narcissist, thrives on creating an environment of dependency, making it difficult for their victim to recognize the unhealthy dynamics at play. Over time, the emotional and psychological toll becomes evident, as the victim experiences confusion, self-doubt, and a profound sense of inadequacy.

The hallmark of a toxic relationship is the consistent erosion of self-worth. Victims may find themselves questioning their reality, trapped in a web of gaslighting and emotional manipulation. The narcissist's need for validation and control can lead to the victim feeling isolated from their support systems, as the abuser often works to alienate them from friends and family. This isolation serves to reinforce the abuser's power, leaving the victim feeling more vulnerable and helpless. The damage caused by such relationships can extend beyond the immediate emotional pain, affecting mental health and overall well-being.

Understanding the characteristics of toxic relationships is crucial for recovery and healing. Signs of toxicity can range from overt aggression and criticism to subtle forms of manipulation and passive-aggressiveness. Recognizing these red flags is the first step toward breaking free from the cycle of abuse. Education about narcissistic traits, such as a lack of empathy, entitlement, and an insatiable need for admiration, equips individuals with the tools to identify unhealthy behaviors. This awareness fosters emotional intelligence, allowing individuals to navigate their relationships more effectively and make informed choices that prioritize their well-being.

Healing from the wounds of toxic relationships requires a commitment to self-discovery and personal growth. It involves understanding one's own emotional triggers and developing strategies for emotional regulation. Techniques such as journaling, meditation, and therapy can provide a safe space for processing trauma and rebuilding self-esteem. The journey to recovery is not linear, but each step taken toward understanding and reclaiming one's power marks a significant victory over the past. With time, patience, and support, individuals can transform their pain into resilience and emerge stronger than before.

The path to empowerment lies in raising awareness about the dynamics of narcissism and the impact of toxic relationships. By sharing experiences and educating others, individuals can foster a culture of emotional health and support. Encouraging open dialogues about the signs of abuse and the importance of emotional intelligence can pave the way for healthier relationships in the future. Together, we can inspire change, heal from trauma, and cultivate a collective understanding that prioritizes empathy, respect, and genuine connection.

You are stronger than you think.
You have survived the impossible.
Now it's time to rise above the pain, embrace your resilience, and create a life that reflects your true worth.

NARCISSISM IN ROMANTIC RELATIONSHIPS

The Allure of the Narcissist

The allure of the narcissist often draws individuals into a captivating yet tumultuous dance, were charm and charisma mask deeper, more troubling traits. At first glance, narcissists can seem magnetic, exuding confidence and a sense of entitlement that can be intoxicating. This initial attraction can lead people to overlook their self-serving behaviors and lack of empathy. Understanding this allure is crucial for anyone seeking to evaluate narcissism, as it highlights the subtle ways in which narcissists can manipulate their environment and the people within it.

Common traits among narcissists include an inflated sense of self-importance, a constant need for admiration, and a profound lack of empathy. These characteristics can be enticing, especially in social or romantic contexts, where confidence is often equated with attractiveness. However, recognizing these traits is essential to understanding the darker implications of engaging with a narcissist. The allure can quickly fade when individuals realize that beneath the surface lies a propensity for emotional manipulation and a tendency to dismiss the feelings of others.

There are various types of narcissists, including grandiose and vulnerable forms, each with unique traits and behaviors. Grandiose narcissists are often the life of the party, reveling in attention and accolades, while vulnerable narcissists may appear shy or insecure but harbor deep-seated feelings of entitlement and victimhood. Understanding these distinctions can empower individuals to navigate relationships more effectively, whether in the realm of romantic partnerships, workplace dynamics, or friendships. Recognizing the type of narcissist, one is dealing with can provide clarity and foster healthier interactions.

Cultural influences also play a significant role in shaping narcissistic behaviors, as societal values often glorify individualism and self-promotion. This cultural backdrop can exacerbate narcissistic tendencies, making it even more challenging to break free from their grasp. For those who find themselves entangled with narcissistic individuals, it's essential to develop strategies for resilience and healing. Recognizing the signs of narcissism, establishing clear boundaries, and seeking support can pave the way toward recovery and personal growth.

Fostering a profound understanding of narcissism requires not only recognizing its allure but also acknowledging the emotional toll it can take on individuals. By learning to identify the traits of narcissists and the impact they have on relationships, people can better equip themselves to distance from harmful dynamics and cultivate healthier connections. Embracing this journey of self-awareness can lead to empowerment, allowing individuals to reclaim their narratives and build relationships that are rooted in mutual respect and genuine care.

Recognizing Toxic Patterns

Recognizing toxic patterns in relationships, whether personal or professional, is crucial for maintaining mental and emotional well-being. Narcissists often exhibit behaviors that can be insidious and difficult to identify at first. They may charm you with their charisma and wit, but as the relationship unfolds, you might start to notice a troubling pattern of manipulation, self-centeredness, and emotional unavailability. Understanding these toxic patterns is the first step toward safeguarding yourself from their pervasive influence and reclaiming your sense of self.

One common pattern is the cycle of:

- **IDEALIZATION**
- **DEVALUATION**
- **DISCARD**

In the initial stages, a narcissist may shower you with attention and affection, making you feel special and valued. However, this phase is often followed by a period of devaluation, where they criticize, belittle, and undermine your self-worth. The final stage, discard, can leave you feeling abandoned and confused, as they move on to the next source of admiration. This cycle is not just damaging; it serves to reinforce their fragile self-esteem while eroding yours.

Another toxic pattern... involves emotional manipulation, often disguised as concern or love. Narcissists frequently employ gaslighting, a tactic that makes you question your reality and perceptions. You might find yourself doubting your own feelings or memories, as they twist situations to fit their narrative. This manipulation can lead to a profound sense of isolation and self-doubt, making it increasingly difficult to recognize the harm being inflicted. By learning to identify these manipulative tactics, you can begin to reclaim your reality and establish stronger boundaries.

In romantic relationships, narcissists may display a lack of empathy, making genuine emotional connection nearly impossible. They often prioritize their needs above all else, leaving their partners feeling neglected and unimportant. This emotional unavailability can lead to a one-sided relationship, where your feelings and needs are consistently overlooked. Recognizing this pattern is essential for your emotional health; it empowers you to seek relationships that offer mutual respect and understanding rather than constant emotional turmoil.

Recognizing toxic patterns is an act of self-love and empowerment. By understanding the signs of narcissism and its harmful effects, you can take proactive steps to protect yourself and foster healthier relationships. Whether it involves distancing yourself from a narcissistic friend, navigating the complexities of a narcissistic parent, or healing after a painful romantic relationship, awareness is the first step toward healing. Embrace the journey of self-discovery, knowing that you have the strength to break free from toxic cycles and cultivate a life filled with genuine connections and emotional well-being.

ESCAPING THE NARCISSIST'S GRIP

Identifying Red Flags

Identifying red flags in relationships with narcissists is crucial for protecting oneself from emotional harm. The first step in this process is to recognize the core traits that are often present in narcissistic individuals. These include an inflated sense of self-importance, a deep need for admiration, and a lack of empathy for others. When someone consistently seeks validation through excessive bragging or dismisses your feelings and needs, it may indicate a narcissistic tendency. Awareness of these traits can empower you to take action before getting entangled in a harmful relationship.

In romantic relationships, spotting red flags can be particularly challenging, as initial charm and charisma often mask underlying issues. A partner who exhibits possessiveness, frequently seeks to control your decisions, or displays extreme jealousy may be exhibiting signs of narcissism. Additionally, if your partner often shifts blame onto you or others, refusing to take responsibility for their actions, it may create a toxic dynamic. Recognizing these behaviors early on can help you avoid the heartache that often accompanies a relationship with a narcissist.

Narcissism isn't confined to romantic relationships; it can also manifest in workplace environments. Identifying red flags at work can safeguard your mental well-being and career growth. Be wary of colleagues or supervisors who take credit for your work, manipulate situations to their advantage, or engage in belittling behavior. These actions not only undermine your contributions but also create a hostile work environment. By being vigilant and understanding these red flags, you can navigate your career path with greater confidence and clarity.

Parenting with a narcissist can be an emotionally draining experience, especially when the parent displays traits that disrupt familial harmony. Children raised by narcissistic parents often find themselves in a cycle of emotional manipulation and invalidation. If a parent consistently prioritizes their own needs over their child's or uses guilt and shame to exert control, this can lead to long-term psychological effects. Understanding these dynamics is essential for breaking the cycle and fostering healthier relationships within the family unit.

Strategies for Distance

Creating distance from a narcissistic individual can be a vital step in reclaiming personal well-being and fostering emotional health. The first strategy involves setting clear boundaries. This means articulating what behaviors are unacceptable and being firm in your resolve to uphold those boundaries. Narcissists often test limits and may react negatively to any perceived challenge to their authority or entitlement. By establishing and maintaining these boundaries, you create a protective space that limits their ability to manipulate or control your emotions and actions.

Another effective strategy is to minimize contact. In situations where complete separation isn't feasible, such as in a workplace or shared parenting scenario, reducing interactions can significantly lessen the emotional toll. This can be achieved through structured communication, where discussions are focused strictly on necessary topics, avoiding personal exchanges that could lead to emotional entanglement. Utilizing technology, such as email or messaging apps, can help keep interactions concise and less emotionally charged, providing a layer of distance that fosters clarity and focus.

Additionally, fostering a support network is paramount. Surrounding yourself with empathetic and understanding individuals serves as a buffer against the manipulative tactics of a narcissist. Friends and family who recognize the challenges posed by narcissistic behavior can provide validation, encouragement, and advice, creating a safe space for you to express your feelings and experiences. This network not only reinforces your sense of self-worth but also reminds you that you are not alone in your journey away from toxicity.

Educating yourself about the nuances of narcissism is also crucial. Understanding the various types of narcissists, from grandiose to vulnerable, and recognizing their common traits can empower you to identify and anticipate potential challenges. Knowledge equips you with the tools to navigate interactions more effectively and helps you recognize when you are being drawn into the narcissist's narrative. This awareness is instrumental in deflecting emotional manipulation and maintaining the distance you need to protect your mental health.

Finally, prioritizing self-care is essential in any strategy for distance. Engaging in activities that promote your physical and emotional well-being can help rebuild your sense of self and reinforce your resilience. Whether through therapy, mindfulness practices, or creative outlets, nurturing yourself creates a foundation of strength that makes it easier to withstand the pressures of a narcissistic relationship. By focusing on your well-being, you not only create a significant distance from the narcissist but also embark on a profound journey of healing and self-discovery.

Building a Support System

Building a support system is crucial for anyone navigating the complexities of narcissism, whether as a victim or an observer. This support system offers not only emotional refuge but also practical guidance. Friends and family who understand the nuances of narcissistic behavior can help validate experiences, provide advice, and, most importantly, remind you of your self-worth when it feels diminished by the narcissist's actions. It is essential to surround yourself with individuals who can see beyond the surface, recognizing the red flags of narcissism and offering informed perspectives on your interactions.

In creating your support network, consider seeking out those who have either experienced similar situations or have educated themselves about narcissism. Support groups, whether in-person or online, provide a space where individuals can share their stories and strategies for coping with narcissistic behavior. These spaces foster understanding and create a sense of community that is vital for healing. Hearing others articulate their experiences can be profoundly reassuring, as it reminds you that you are not alone in your struggles and that there are effective ways to cope and move forward.

Equally important is the inclusion of mental health professionals in your support system. Therapists who specialize in narcissistic abuse can equip you with the tools to recognize and counteract emotional manipulation. They can guide you through the process of rebuilding your self-esteem and developing assertiveness. Engaging with professionals allows for a deeper exploration of how narcissism operates within relationships and equips you with strategies to protect yourself, whether it be in romantic engagements, workplace dynamics, or even in familial settings.

Your support system should also include self-care practices that reinforce your emotional well-being. Activities such as journaling, meditation, or engaging in creative outlets can serve as powerful tools for reflection and healing. They allow you to process your experiences and reaffirm your identity outside of the narcissist's influence. By prioritizing self-care, you cultivate resilience that not only helps you withstand the narcissistic behaviors of others but also promotes a healthier mindset as you heal.

Ultimately, building a support system is about reclaiming your narrative and fostering connections grounded in empathy and understanding. By surrounding yourself with those who uplift you and provide a safe space for expression, you empower yourself to not only recognize narcissistic traits in others but also to navigate your interactions with confidence. This support not only aids in recovery but also strengthens your ability to foster healthy relationships moving forward, ensuring that the impact of narcissism does not define your life.

Breaking Free from Toxic Relationships

Breaking free from toxic relationships often feels like scaling a mountain, with every step forward met by the weight of the past dragging you down. Understanding the nature of narcissistic abuse and the trauma bonds that form can empower you to reclaim your life. It is crucial to recognize that these bonds, while deeply ingrained, can be severed. By acknowledging the emotional entanglement and the psychological manipulation that defines these relationships, you are already on the path to liberation. Remember, the journey may be challenging, but it is entirely possible to emerge stronger and more resilient than before.

The first step to breaking free is recognizing the signs of a toxic relationship. Narcissistic partners often employ tactics that lead to confusion, self-doubt, and emotional exhaustion. They may oscillate between intense love and cold indifference, creating an unhealthy cycle that leaves you questioning your worth. Acknowledging these patterns is vital. It allows you to name the chaos, understand the dynamics at play, and begin to detach your sense of self from the narcissist's distorted reality. This clarity is the beginning of your empowerment, as you learn that you are not to blame for the abuse you endured.

Once you have identified the toxicity, the real work begins: dismantling the trauma bond. This process involves recognizing the emotional and psychological hooks that have kept you tethered to your abuser. It requires a commitment to self-care and healing, which may include therapy, support groups, or journaling. As you engage in these practices, you will start to rediscover your identity outside of the relationship. Embrace the discomfort of this journey; it is a sign that you are breaking away from the familiar patterns that once dictated your life. Each day you choose to prioritize your well-being over the toxic relationship is a step toward reclaiming your power.

Post-traumatic growth is not just a possibility; it is a reality for many who have endured narcissistic abuse. As you navigate the aftermath, allow yourself to envision a future filled with hope and potential. The trauma you experienced doesn't define you; instead, it can serve as a catalyst for profound personal transformation. By confronting your pain, you can cultivate resilience and discover new strengths. Surround yourself with supportive individuals who encourage your growth and celebrate your victories, no matter how small. Each success, whether it's setting boundaries or engaging in healthy relationships, reinforces your journey toward healing.

Lastly, as you break free from toxic relationships, remember that PTSD is not merely a disorder; it is an injury that requires care and attention. Approaching your healing process with this mindset can shift how you perceive your experiences and the resources you seek for recovery. Embrace therapies that resonate with you, whether they are traditional or alternative, and allow yourself to explore new coping mechanisms. By treating your PTSD with the seriousness it deserves, you lay the groundwork for a life beyond the shadows of the past. Your story is one of resilience, and by breaking free from the chains of narcissistic abuse, you are writing a new chapter filled with empowerment, healing, and hope.

Narcissistic abuse can erode your sense of self-worth, but healing is about reclaiming your power, rediscovering your voice, and redefining your own narrative.

You are not defined by your past experiences with narcissistic abuse. You are strong, resilient, and capable of healing. Embrace your journey, celebrate your progress, and remember that you are worthy of love and happiness.

Managing PTSD and Suicidal Thoughts from Narcissistic Abuse

AFTERMATH OF A NARCISSISTIC RELATIONSHIP

The Damage Left Behind

The aftermath of a relationship with a narcissist can leave deep, often invisible scars that affect every facet of an individual's life. Survivors frequently grapple with emotional turmoil, self-doubt, and a pervasive sense of unworthiness. The damage extends far beyond the end of the relationship, as the insidious effects of manipulation and control linger long after the narcissist has exited the stage. This emotional residue can manifest in anxiety, depression, and difficulties in trusting others, making the journey toward healing an essential, yet challenging endeavor.

In the wake of narcissistic abuse, many individuals find themselves questioning their reality and the validity of their feelings. The gaslighting often employed by narcissists serves to obscure the truth, leaving victims confused and isolated. They may struggle with emotional regulation, feeling as if they are on an unpredictable rollercoaster of highs and lows. Understanding that this confusion is a direct result of manipulation can be the first step toward reclaiming one's sense of self. Knowledge becomes a powerful tool in dismantling the false narratives that have been imposed, allowing survivors to begin the process of recovery.

Healing from the damage inflicted by a narcissist requires a multifaceted approach that prioritizes emotional intelligence. Building this skill set involves recognizing one's emotions, understanding their origins, and learning to respond rather than react. Techniques such as mindfulness and self-reflection can help survivors gain clarity and develop healthier coping mechanisms. Additionally, seeking support from therapists or support groups can provide validation and understanding, creating a safe space for survivors to share their experiences and begin the healing process.

The journey of recovery is not linear; it is fraught with setbacks and moments of doubt. However, each step taken toward reclaiming one's emotional health is a testament to resilience. By actively working to rebuild self-esteem and establishing boundaries, survivors can transform their experiences into sources of empowerment. Engaging in activities that promote self-care and personal growth can further facilitate this transformation, fostering a renewed sense of purpose and joy that transcends past trauma.

Ultimately, the damage left behind by a narcissist does not have to define the future. With commitment to self-discovery and healing, individuals can rise from the ashes of toxic relationships, equipped with the emotional intelligence needed to foster positive connections with others. By embracing their journey and sharing their stories, survivors can not only find their voice but also inspire others to confront the shadows of narcissistic abuse, paving the way for a collective awakening and a deeper understanding of emotional health.

Recognizing PTSD Symptoms

Recognizing the symptoms of PTSD is a crucial step in reclaiming your life after the emotional turmoil of a relationship with a narcissist. Often, the signs of this condition can be subtle and easily dismissed, especially in the aftermath of an emotionally draining experience. Common symptoms include persistent feelings of anxiety and depression, flashbacks to traumatic events, and an overwhelming sense of guilt or shame. Understanding these symptoms is essential for individuals who have endured narcissistic abuse, as they highlight the profound impact such relationships can have on mental health. Acknowledging these feelings is not a sign of weakness but rather a courageous step toward healing.

One of the hallmark symptoms of PTSD is hypervigilance, where you find yourself constantly on edge, anticipating danger even when it is not present. This heightened state of awareness is often a response to the unpredictability of living with a narcissist. You may also experience emotional numbness, a common defense mechanism that can leave you feeling disconnected from your emotions and those around you. Recognizing this symptom is vital, as it signifies a protective barrier you have constructed to shield yourself from further pain. Understanding that these reactions are normal responses to trauma can help you approach your healing journey with compassion.

Flashbacks and intrusive memories can also be prevalent in individuals dealing with PTSD stemming from narcissistic abuse. These episodes can manifest unexpectedly, often triggered by seemingly innocuous details that remind you of past experiences. It's important to recognize that these flashbacks are not just memories; they are reminders of your resilience in the face of chaos. By identifying these moments, you can begin to process them in a safe environment, allowing yourself to confront the pain without being overwhelmed. This recognition is a powerful tool in dismantling the trauma bond that may still hold you captive.

Suicidal ideation is another critical symptom that deserves immediate attention. The despair that can accompany PTSD can lead to feelings of hopelessness, making it essential to understand that these thoughts do not define your worth or your future. Recognizing these thoughts as a symptom of your trauma rather than a reflection of your reality is a key step toward recovery. It is crucial to seek support, whether through therapy, support groups, or trusted individuals in your life, as reaching out can be a lifeline in moments of darkness. You are not alone, and there are pathways to healing that can lead you back to a place of hope.

Redefining PTSD as an injury rather than a disorder can empower you on your healing journey. This perspective encourages you to treat yourself with the same care and compassion you would offer someone recovering from a physical injury. By recognizing the symptoms of PTSD as signals from your body that require attention, you can begin to develop effective coping mechanisms tailored to your unique experience. Embracing post-traumatic growth means finding strength in your vulnerability and transforming your pain into resilience. As you learn to recognize and address your PTSD symptoms, you embark on a path not just of survival but of thriving after the chaos of narcissistic abuse.

The Cycle of Depression and Anxiety

The cycle of depression and anxiety often emerges as a direct consequence of the emotional turmoil inflicted by narcissistic relationships. Individuals entangled in toxic dynamics may find themselves trapped in a repetitive loop of despair, where moments of fleeting hope are overshadowed by overwhelming feelings of inadequacy and fear. This cycle is not simply a byproduct of personal weakness; rather, it is a profound response to the relentless emotional strain of living under the influence of a narcissist. Recognizing this cycle is the first step towards breaking free and reclaiming one's sense of self-worth.

At the core of this cycle lies the trauma bond, a psychological phenomenon that entwines victims in a harmful attachment to their abuser. This bond can exacerbate feelings of anxiety and depression, making it challenging to detach from the relationship, even when it is clearly detrimental. The initial highs of affection and validation are often followed by periods of manipulation and emotional deprivation, creating a seesaw of emotions that leaves individuals feeling confused and helpless. Understanding this dynamic is crucial; it allows survivors to see that their emotional responses are not indicative of their character, but rather a natural reaction to an unnatural situation.

As the cycle continues, the symptoms of PTSD become increasingly pronounced, manifesting as heightened anxiety, intrusive thoughts, and a pervasive sense of hopelessness. It is essential to shift the perspective on PTSD from being a mere disorder to recognizing it as an injury that requires care and attention. Just as one would tend to a physical injury, individuals must learn to address their emotional wounds with the same urgency and compassion. This reframing empowers survivors to seek treatment and develop coping mechanisms that honor their experiences rather than diminish them.

Breaking the cycle involves a multifaceted approach that encompasses self-awareness, healing practices, and the cultivation of supportive relationships. Engaging in therapy can provide a safe space to process trauma and develop strategies to manage anxiety and depressive symptoms. Moreover, surrounding oneself with understanding individuals who validate one's feelings can foster resilience and a stronger sense of community. It is within this supportive environment that survivors can begin to dismantle the trauma bond and rediscover their intrinsic value.

Ultimately, the journey through the cycle of depression and anxiety can lead to profound personal growth and transformation. By embracing the complexities of their experiences, individuals can emerge from the shadows of narcissistic abuse with newfound strength and clarity. This post-traumatic growth is not only possible but can serve as a testament to the resilience of the human spirit.

As survivors reclaim their lives, they become beacons of hope for others, illustrating that, while the path may be fraught with challenges, it is also rich with opportunities for healing and empowerment.

IDENTIFYING SUICIDAL IDEATION

The Reality of Suicidal Ideation

The experience of suicidal ideation often emerges as a shadowy consequence of the emotional turmoil inflicted by narcissistic abuse. For many, the aftermath of such relationships is marked by deep psychological scars that can lead to feelings of hopelessness and despair. This reality is not just a fleeting thought but a tangible experience that signifies a profound struggle against the remnants of trauma. Recognizing that these thoughts are a symptom of the injury caused by narcissistic abuse is crucial. It is a reminder that the pain is valid and deserves attention and care, much like any physical injury would.

Understanding the nature of suicidal ideation within the context of PTSD is vital for those who have endured the emotional drain of a narcissistic relationship. The trauma bond can create a cycle of dependency, making it difficult to break free from the clutches of toxic dynamics. This bond often leads to feelings of isolation and worthlessness, which can exacerbate depressive symptoms and intensify suicidal thoughts. Acknowledging these feelings as part of the healing process is essential. It is a recognition that these thoughts do not define one's worth but are rather a call for help and understanding.

Breaking free from this cycle requires a multifaceted approach. It is important to cultivate a support system that acknowledges the severity of the trauma and the resulting mental health challenges.

Therapy can play a pivotal role in unpacking the layers of emotional pain and creating a safe space for healing. Through the therapeutic process, individuals can learn to identify triggers and develop coping mechanisms that empower them to manage suicidal thoughts more effectively. This journey toward healing is not linear, but strides made in understanding and addressing these thoughts can pave the way for resilience.

Post-traumatic growth can emerge from the depths of despair. While suicidal ideation may seem insurmountable, it can also serve as a catalyst for transformation. Many individuals find strength in their vulnerability, using their experiences to foster empathy and connection with others who have faced similar struggles. This shared understanding can cultivate a sense of community and hope, highlighting that recovery is not only possible but can lead to a more profound appreciation for life and its complexities.

Ultimately, redefining PTSD as an injury rather than a disorder can shift the perspective for many who have endured narcissistic abuse. This paradigm shift encourages individuals to seek the care and validation they deserve, acknowledging that healing is a process that requires time and patience. Embracing this journey, with all its ups and downs, can lead to a newfound sense of purpose and empowerment. By confronting the reality of suicidal ideation and the trauma that fuels it, individuals can reclaim their narrative and emerge stronger, ready to thrive beyond the chaos.

Understanding Suicidal Thoughts

Understanding suicidal thoughts is a critical aspect of addressing the aftermath of narcissistic abuse. For many who have endured the emotional turmoil inflicted by a narcissistic partner, these thoughts can emerge as a byproduct of persistent trauma. It is essential to recognize that experiencing suicidal ideation does not imply weakness or failure; rather, it signals a profound need for healing and support. This understanding empowers individuals to seek help while validating their feelings as legitimate responses to their painful experiences.

The trauma bond formed in relationships with narcissists can create a complex psychological landscape. This bond often leads to confusion and internal conflict, where love and pain intertwine. In this context, suicidal thoughts may arise as a desperate attempt to escape overwhelming emotions or as a misguided belief that death is the only way to end the suffering. Breaking free from this bond involves recognizing the manipulation and emotional abuse that fueled it, allowing survivors to reclaim their autonomy and begin the healing process.

The emotional and psychological scars left by narcissistic abuse can manifest in various ways, including anxiety, depression, and suicidal ideation. Understanding that Post-Traumatic Stress Disorder (PTSD) should be viewed not as a disorder but as an injury helps individuals acknowledge their experience as a valid response to trauma. By treating PTSD as an injury, survivors can develop a more compassionate relationship with themselves, fostering a mindset conducive to recovery and growth.

Coping mechanisms play a pivotal role in managing the symptoms of PTSD and suicidal thoughts. Techniques such as mindfulness, grounding exercises, and creative expression can provide immediate relief and foster resilience. Additionally, seeking professional help through therapy can offer tools to navigate the complexities of trauma and emotional pain. Engaging in supportive communities, whether in-person or online, can also create connections that remind individuals they are not alone in their struggles. Each step taken towards managing these thoughts is a testament to personal strength and a commitment to healing.

Ultimately, the journey towards understanding and overcoming suicidal thoughts is intertwined with the process of post-traumatic growth. While the aftermath of narcissistic abuse can feel insurmountable, it is possible to emerge from the darkness stronger and more resilient. By redefining the narrative around PTSD and recognizing the potential for growth, individuals can transform their experiences into a source of empowerment. This journey is not linear, but with patience, support, and self-compassion, it is possible to thrive beyond the pain and reclaim a sense of purpose and joy in life.

Recognizing Triggers and Warning Signs

Recognizing triggers and warning signs is a crucial step in managing the complexities of PTSD and suicidal thoughts that often arise after experiencing narcissistic abuse. Triggers can come in many forms: a specific phrase, a tone of voice, or even a particular setting that reminds you of past trauma. Understanding these triggers can empower you to anticipate and mitigate their effects. Keeping a journal can be an invaluable tool in this process, allowing you to document your experiences and identify patterns. By acknowledging these moments, you are taking the first step toward reclaiming your life and understanding the emotional landscape you navigate daily.

Warning signs often manifest as changes in mood, behavior, or physical health. You may notice increased irritability, withdrawal from social interactions, or a resurgence of anxiety and depression. Recognizing these signs early can prevent a downward spiral and provide an opportunity to reach out for help. It is essential to develop a personal action plan that includes coping strategies, supportive contacts, and professional resources. When you can identify these signs, you empower yourself to take proactive measures that honor your emotional well-being and foster resilience.

Establishing a routine that incorporates self-care can help create a sense of stability in an otherwise chaotic emotional environment. This might include regular exercise, mindfulness practices, or engaging in hobbies that bring you joy. When you nurture yourself, you build a buffer against the impact of triggers and warning signs. Surrounding yourself with supportive individuals who understand your journey will also fortify your resilience. Remember, you are not alone in this struggle; many have walked this path and emerged stronger, proving that healing is not only possible but also a deeply rewarding journey.

Understanding the connection between your feelings and the aftermath of narcissistic abuse is paramount. The trauma bonds formed in these toxic relationships can complicate the healing process, often leading to feelings of guilt or self-blame. Breaking free from these bonds requires patience and self-compassion. Embrace the knowledge that your feelings are valid and that recognizing them is a sign of strength. This journey may be challenging, but it is also an opportunity for profound personal growth. Each step you take toward understanding your triggers and warning signs is a step toward liberation from the emotional chains that bind you.

Finally, redefining PTSD as an injury rather than a disorder can shift your perspective and encourage a more compassionate approach to healing. This reframing allows you to view your experiences through the lens of recovery and resilience. Just as one would seek treatment for any physical injury, you have the right to seek help for your emotional wounds. There is hope and light on the other side of this struggle. By recognizing your triggers and warning signs, you are not just surviving; you are actively engaging in a process that can lead to thriving after trauma. Embrace this journey as a testament to your strength and a pathway to a brighter future.

Developing a Safety Plan

Developing a safety plan is an essential step in reclaiming your life after the chaos of narcissistic abuse. It serves as a proactive measure, providing a structured approach to navigate through potential crises and overwhelming emotions. The first step in creating this plan is to identify your triggers—those specific situations, thoughts, or interactions that evoke distressing feelings or thoughts of self-harm. By acknowledging these triggers, you empower yourself to take control of your environment and emotional responses. Write down these triggers and reflect on how they impact your mental well-being. This awareness will be your first line of defense in protecting your emotional health.

Next, establish a list of coping mechanisms that resonate with you. These can range from mindfulness practices to physical activities, or even creative outlets like journaling or art. The goal is to create a toolkit filled with strategies that soothe and ground you during moments of crisis. Experiment with different techniques to find what works best for you. Remember, what may bring comfort to one person might not be effective for another, so tailor your list to your unique preferences and needs. This personalized toolkit will become invaluable as you work through the challenges of PTSD and emotional turmoil.

1. Incorporating a support system into your safety plan is vital. Identify individuals in your life who understand your journey and can offer encouragement and support. This could be friends, family members, or mental health professionals who can provide a listening ear or constructive advice when needed. Clearly communicate your feelings with these trusted individuals, and don't hesitate to reach out when you feel overwhelmed. Establishing a network of support not only helps

you feel less isolated but also strengthens your resilience as you navigate the aftermath of narcissistic abuse.

2. Outline actionable steps to take when you find yourself feeling vulnerable. This could include specific phone numbers to call, places to go, or activities to engage in that can help redirect your thoughts. Whether it's taking a walk in nature, attending a support group, or simply reaching out for a chat, having these steps outlined ensures you are prepared to act when emotions surge. Consistency is key; the more you practice these actions, the more natural they will become, reinforcing your ability to cope with distress.

3. Regularly review and update your safety plan as your healing progresses. Your needs and coping strategies may evolve, and it's essential to adapt your plan accordingly. Celebrate the small victories along your journey, recognizing that healing from the trauma of narcissistic abuse is a gradual process. By developing a safety plan, you are not only protecting yourself but also actively participating in your own recovery. Embrace this journey, knowing that you have the power to reclaim your life and emerge stronger than before.

Redefining PTSD

PTSD AS AN INJURY

Understanding PTSD Beyond a Disorder

Understanding PTSD extends far beyond the confines of a clinical diagnosis; it is a profound acknowledgment of the emotional and psychological injuries that individuals endure, particularly following experiences of narcissistic abuse. When navigating the aftermath of such toxic relationships, it is vital to recognize that PTSD is not merely a disorder but an injury that requires compassionate care and healing. This perspective shifts the narrative from one of shame and stigma to empowerment and resilience. By redefining PTSD in this manner, survivors can begin to understand their experiences as valid and worthy of treatment, much like any physical injury.

The essence of PTSD lies in its roots in trauma bonds, which can form in the chaotic dynamics of narcissistic relationships. These bonds create a cycle of emotional dependency and confusion, where the victim becomes entwined in the abuser's manipulative patterns. Understanding this phenomenon is crucial for breaking free from the chains of emotional abuse. Recognizing the trauma bond allows individuals to confront the reality of their experiences and to realize that their emotional turmoil is a legitimate response to a harmful relationship. This clarity is a pivotal first step toward healing, empowering survivors to reclaim their autonomy and redefine their identity outside of the abusive framework.

Many individuals who have experienced narcissistic abuse find that their journey through PTSD can lead to profound personal development and insight. This growth does not diminish the pain endured but rather highlights the strength and resilience that can emerge from such adversity. Survivors may discover new facets of themselves, develop healthier relationships, and cultivate a deeper understanding of their emotional needs. By focusing on the possibility of post-traumatic growth, individuals can shift their mindset from victimhood to empowerment, embracing the journey as one of discovery and renewal.

Coping mechanisms are essential tools for managing the effects of PTSD resulting from narcissistic abuse. These mechanisms can range from mindfulness practices and therapy to building a supportive community of understanding individuals. It is crucial for survivors to explore various strategies that resonate with them and to prioritize self-care as part of their healing journey. Seeking professional help, engaging in creative outlets, and practicing grounding techniques can assist in navigating the complex emotions tied to PTSD. Each small step taken in the direction of healing is a testament to the survivor's strength and commitment to their well-being.

Lastly, addressing suicidal ideation is an essential component of the recovery process. Survivors of narcissistic abuse often grapple with overwhelming feelings of despair and hopelessness. By openly discussing these thoughts and feelings, individuals can begin to dismantle the shame associated with them. It is vital to create a safe space where survivors feel heard and supported, allowing them to express their struggles without fear of judgment. By emphasizing the importance of seeking help and connecting with others, we can foster an environment that nurtures healing and resilience. Understanding PTSD as an injury rather than a disorder not only validates the survivor's experience but also paves the way for a compassionate approach to recovery.

Viewing PTSD as an Injury

Post-Traumatic Stress Disorder (PTSD) is often mischaracterized as merely a mental health disorder, but this perspective can diminish the profound impact it has on individuals, especially those recovering from narcissistic abuse. When we shift our understanding of PTSD to view it as an injury, we begin to recognize the significance of the trauma endured and the need for recovery akin to physical healing. Just as a broken bone requires time, care, and rehabilitation, so too does the mind require intentional nurturing and support after experiencing the emotional wounds inflicted by narcissistic relationships.

Understanding PTSD as an injury allows individuals to acknowledge their pain without the stigma often associated with mental health disorders. This perspective empowers survivors to validate their experiences and emotions, creating a foundation for healing. Just like any physical injury, the path to recovery involves identifying the source of the pain, accepting its existence, and committing to a process of healing. By reframing PTSD in this way, individuals can embrace their journey toward recovery, knowing that it is not only permissible but essential to prioritize their mental health as they would their physical health.

In recognizing PTSD as an injury, it becomes clear that adequate treatment is essential for recovery. This treatment may take various forms, including therapy, support groups, and self-care practices that nourish the body and mind. It is crucial to engage in a holistic approach that addresses the emotional, social, and psychological aspects of healing. Just as one would follow a prescribed regimen for a physical injury, those suffering from PTSD must seek out resources and strategies tailored to their specific needs, ensuring that their journey is both supported and effective.

1. Viewing PTSD as an injury underscores the importance of understanding trauma bonds and the aftermath of toxic relationships. Individuals often feel as though they are trapped in a cycle of pain and confusion, struggling to break free from the grip of their abuser. Recognizing that these bonds can lead to significant emotional and psychological injuries empowers survivors to take actionable steps toward liberation. Education about the dynamics of narcissism and its effects on mental health can serve as a catalyst for change, encouraging individuals to seek the help they need to untangle themselves from these detrimental connections.
2. The process of healing from PTSD resulting from narcissistic abuse is not only about surviving but thriving. By

redefining PTSD as an injury in need of care, individuals can cultivate resilience and post-traumatic growth. This journey involves not only recovering from the wounds of the past but also embracing the opportunity for personal development, strength, and newfound purpose. As survivors navigate this path, they can transform their experiences into a powerful narrative of survival, emerging with a deeper understanding of themselves and a commitment to living a fulfilling life beyond the shadows of their trauma

The IMPORTANCE of Treating PTSD as an Injury

Understanding PTSD as an injury rather than merely a disorder is pivotal in reshaping how we approach healing from the aftermath of narcissistic abuse. This shift in perspective encourages individuals to view their experiences through a lens of resilience rather than deficiency. Just as a physical injury demands attention and care, so too does the emotional and psychological toll that PTSD exacts on a person. Recognizing PTSD as an injury emphasizes the seriousness of the trauma endured and advocates for the necessity of comprehensive treatment and support systems tailored to the needs of survivors.

When we treat PTSD as an injury, we validate the pain and struggles faced by those affected. Survivors of narcissistic abuse often grapple with feelings of shame, isolation, and confusion, which can be compounded by societal misconceptions about mental health. By framing PTSD as an injury, we foster an environment where individuals can openly discuss their experiences without fear of judgment or stigmatization. This validation is crucial in the healing process, as it allows survivors to acknowledge their suffering and seek the appropriate care they deserve.

Moreover, treating PTSD as an injury underscores the importance of a multidisciplinary approach to recovery. Just as one might require physical therapy, medication, or rehabilitation after an injury, those dealing with PTSD need a comprehensive array of support options. This can include therapy, peer support groups, and self-care practices tailored to individual needs. Such an approach empowers survivors to take an active role in their healing journey, equipping them with the tools necessary to navigate the complexities of their trauma and emerge stronger.

The journey of healing from PTSD can also lead to post-traumatic growth, a phenomenon that is often overlooked. When individuals take the time to address their trauma as an injury, they can uncover newfound strengths and insights about themselves and their relationships. This growth can manifest in various ways, such as enhanced empathy, a greater appreciation for life, and the ability to foster healthier connections. Embracing this perspective allows survivors to transform their pain into a catalyst for personal development and resilience.

Ultimately, redefining PTSD as an injury reinforces the notion that healing is not only possible but also a transformative journey. It inspires individuals to reclaim their lives and break free from the trauma bonds that have held them captive. This shift in understanding encourages a proactive stance on mental health, promoting self-compassion and the pursuit of holistic healing methods. By embracing the idea that PTSD is an injury in need of care, we affirm that recovery is not just a distant hope but a tangible reality waiting to be realized.

Be patient with yourself, celebrate your progress, and never give up on your journey of self-discovery and healing.

POST-TRAUMATIC GROWTH

The Concept of Post-Traumatic Growth

The concept of post-traumatic growth offers a powerful perspective for individuals who have endured the ravages of narcissistic abuse and its resulting trauma. Rather than viewing PTSD solely as a debilitating disorder, it can be reframed as an injury that, with the right care and attention, can lead to profound personal transformation. This growth often emerges from the ashes of suffering, revealing hidden strengths and newfound insights that can guide individuals toward a more resilient and fulfilling life. Those who have experienced the chaos of narcissistic relationships may find that the very struggles they face can also become steppingstones toward healing and self-discovery.

Post-traumatic growth unfolds in various dimensions, including an increased appreciation for life, deeper relationships, and a heightened sense of personal strength. Individuals may notice a shift in their priorities, choosing to engage more deeply with the world around them. This newfound clarity can serve as a catalyst for change, prompting individuals to let go of toxic patterns and embrace healthier connections. The journey toward growth is not linear, and it often requires navigating the complex emotions that accompany recovery. However, those willing to confront their pain can emerge with a richer understanding of themselves and their capabilities.

Breaking free from trauma bonds is an essential aspect of this growth process. When entangled in a relationship with a narcissist, individuals often find themselves caught in a cycle of emotional manipulation and dependency. Recognizing the patterns of these bonds is a crucial step in reclaiming one's autonomy. By fostering self-awareness and practicing self-compassion, individuals can begin to dismantle the emotional chains that have held them captive. This liberation is not merely an escape; it is an opportunity to redefine one's identity and purpose, ultimately paving the way for a more authentic and empowered existence.

Coping mechanisms play a pivotal role in facilitating post-traumatic growth. Engaging in therapeutic practices, such as mindfulness, journaling, and support groups, can provide individuals with essential tools for processing their experiences. These strategies not only promote emotional regulation but also nurture a sense of community and connection with others who have faced similar struggles. By actively participating in their healing journey, individuals can cultivate resilience and foster a mindset that embraces growth amidst adversity. The process may be challenging, yet it is through these challenges that the seeds of transformation can take root.

The link between narcissism, trauma, and mental health is profound, yet it is not insurmountable. Embracing the concept of post-traumatic growth allows individuals to shift their focus from victimhood to empowerment. Each step taken on the path of healing holds the potential for renewal and strength. The journey may be fraught with difficulties, but by recognizing the possibility of growth after trauma, individuals can foster hope and resilience in their lives. In this way, the narrative of pain can be rewritten into one of triumph and inspiration, illuminating the way for others who seek to heal and thrive after the storm of narcissistic abuse.

Healing from a Narcissistic Partner

Healing from a narcissistic partner requires a deep understanding of the emotional turmoil that accompanies such relationships. The journey often begins with recognizing the patterns of manipulation, emotional abuse, and control that may have been normalized during the partnership. Acknowledge the pain and confusion; these feelings are valid and indicative of the struggles faced. By identifying the traits common to narcissists, such as a lack of empathy, a constant need for admiration, and a tendency to belittle others, individuals can begin to distance themselves from the toxic dynamics that have caused harm.

Once awareness is established, the next step involves setting firm boundaries. This is crucial not only for personal safety but also for emotional recovery. Boundaries serve as a protective barrier against further manipulation and emotional depletion. Individuals must learn to prioritize their own needs and feelings, understanding that it is not selfish to do so. Establishing these limits can be challenging, especially when ingrained patterns of people-pleasing have been developed, but it is essential for reclaiming personal power and fostering self-respect.

Support from others plays a vital role in the healing process. Engaging with friends, family, or support groups can provide a sense of community and understanding that diminishes feelings of isolation. Sharing experiences with those who have encountered similar situations can be incredibly validating and can reinforce the notion that recovery is not only possible but also a shared journey. Professional counseling or therapy can also be invaluable, offering tools and strategies to confront the emotional scars left by a narcissistic partner.

Self-reflection and self-compassion are powerful instruments in the healing toolkit. Taking time to process the relationship and its impact allows individuals to recognize their own worth, which may have been diminished during the partnership. Journaling, meditation, or creative expression can facilitate this introspective work. Embracing one's feelings, rather than suppressing them, can lead to profound insights and a stronger sense of self. This period of self-discovery is a crucial transition from victimhood to empowerment.

Ultimately, healing from a narcissistic partner is a journey of transformation. It is not merely about moving on; it is about evolving into a stronger, more resilient individual. By understanding the complexities of narcissism and the ways it permeates relationships, individuals can gain clarity and confidence. This newfound awareness not only aids in personal recovery but also equips them with the knowledge to recognize and avoid similar patterns in the future. Embracing this path can lead to healthier relationships, both with oneself and with others, creating a life filled with genuine connections and emotional fulfillment.

Strategies for Healing

Healing from the aftermath of narcissistic abuse is a journey that requires patience, resilience, and the right strategies to foster recovery. Understanding that PTSD is not merely a disorder but an injury that demands care is essential. This perspective allows individuals to approach their healing with the intention and dedication that one would apply to a physical injury. Recognizing the symptoms of trauma and how they manifest in daily life is the first step in developing a comprehensive healing strategy. By acknowledging these experiences, individuals can begin to navigate their emotional landscape with greater clarity and purpose.

1. One effective strategy for healing is establishing a robust support system. Connecting with others who have similar experiences can be incredibly validating and comforting. Support groups, whether in-person or online, offer a safe space to share stories and feelings without judgment. Additionally, engaging with friends and family who are empathetic can provide essential emotional support. This network not only fosters a sense of belonging but also helps to dismantle the isolation that often accompanies trauma. By

cultivating these relationships, individuals can gradually build a foundation of trust and safety that is crucial for healing.

2. Another crucial strategy involves the practice of self-compassion and mindfulness. Individuals recovering from narcissistic abuse often struggle with feelings of guilt, shame, and self-blame. By intentionally practicing self-compassion, individuals can begin to reframe their internal dialogues, treating themselves with the kindness they would offer a friend in similar circumstances. Mindfulness techniques, such as meditation and deep breathing exercises, can also help ground individuals in the present moment, reducing anxiety and fostering emotional regulation. These practices encourage a deeper connection with oneself, which is vital for overcoming the trauma bond formed in toxic relationships.

Incorporating creative outlets into the healing process can also be transformative. Art, writing, music, or any form of self-expression allows individuals to process their emotions and experiences in a constructive way. Engaging in creative activities can serve as a powerful form of catharsis, helping to articulate feelings that may be difficult to express verbally. This exploration not only aids in understanding the complexities of one's emotions but also fosters a sense of agency and empowerment. As individuals create, they reclaim their narratives and redefine their identities beyond the confines of past trauma.

Embracing the concept of post-traumatic growth is essential. While the aftermath of narcissistic abuse can leave deep scars, it can also serve as a catalyst for profound personal transformation. By reflecting on the lessons learned and the strengths gained through adversity, individuals can cultivate a renewed sense of purpose and resilience. This growth mindset encourages a shift from merely surviving to thriving, allowing individuals to envision a future filled with possibilities. By implementing these strategies—building support networks, practicing self-compassion, engaging in creative expression, and fostering a growth mindset—healing becomes not only attainable but also a profound journey of rediscovery and empowerment.

Thriving After Toxic Relationships

Emerging from the shadows of a toxic relationship can feel like stepping into an entirely new world. The journey of healing after the emotional turmoil inflicted by a narcissist is undeniably challenging, yet it offers the potential for profound transformation. It is essential to recognize that thriving after such experiences is not only possible but also a testament to your resilience and strength. This chapter aims to illuminate the path to recovery, focusing on the opportunities for growth and renewal that await you.

Understanding the intricacies of trauma bonds is a critical first step towards liberation. These bonds often create a cycle of emotional dependency that can be incredibly difficult to break. However, acknowledging the manipulative patterns at play empowers you to reclaim your narrative. It is vital to view this process as an act of self-love. Each step taken towards disentangling yourself from the past is a powerful affirmation of your worth and your right to experience healthy, fulfilling relationships. Embrace this journey as a chance to redefine your identity outside of the constraints imposed by your abuser.

Post-traumatic growth is a remarkable phenomenon that can arise from the ashes of pain. As you navigate the aftermath of your experience, you may discover newfound strengths and insights that you never knew existed within you. This growth often manifests as a deeper understanding of yourself, enhanced empathy, and a clearer sense of what you want and deserve in life. By reframing your PTSD not as a disorder, but as an injury that requires care and attention, you open yourself up to healing practices that nurture your mind, body, and spirit. This perspective shift is integral to developing a healthier relationship with your past.

Coping mechanisms play a significant role in your recovery journey. Engaging in mindfulness, journaling, or creative expression can provide essential outlets for processing your emotions. Surrounding yourself with a supportive community fosters an environment where vulnerability is met with compassion rather than judgment. It is crucial to remember that healing is not linear; there will be ups and downs. However, each effort you make towards self-care and connection brings you closer to a life marked by joy and purpose, rather than fear and anxiety.

Thriving after toxic relationships is about reclaiming your narrative and embracing the possibilities that lie ahead. Your journey is unique, and it deserves to be honored. As you navigate the complexities of healing, remember that you have the power to redefine your story. Embrace the lessons learned, the strength gained, and the hope that blossoms from your experiences.

You are not defined by your past but by your ability to rise, rebuild, and flourish in a life that reflects your true self.

Building Resilience and Hope

Building resilience and hope in the aftermath of narcissistic abuse is a transformative journey that requires strength and perseverance. It begins with recognizing that the emotional scars left by such relationships are not just fleeting feelings but deeply rooted injuries that deserve attention and care. Acknowledging that PTSD is an injury, not a disorder, empowers individuals to approach their healing with intention and purpose. This perspective shifts the narrative from one of victimhood to one of empowerment, allowing survivors to reclaim their narratives and take active steps toward recovery.

Understanding trauma bonds is crucial in this process. These bonds often create a confusing mix of attachment and distress, leaving individuals feeling trapped in a cycle of emotional turmoil. Breaking free from these toxic relationships involves recognizing the patterns that have kept them ensnared. It is essential to identify the signs of emotional manipulation and to understand that healing requires not only detachment from the abuser but also a commitment to self-discovery and self-love. Each step taken away from the narcissistic influence is a step toward building a resilient foundation for a healthier future.

Post-traumatic growth illustrates how individuals can thrive after experiencing profound trauma. While the journey may be riddled with setbacks, it also presents opportunities for personal development and strength. Survivors can harness their experiences to cultivate resilience and gain insights that enrich their lives. By focusing on what has been learned through adversity, individuals can foster a renewed sense of purpose and hope. This growth is not linear; it is filled with ups and downs, but every small victory contributes to the overall healing process.

Coping mechanisms play a vital role in managing the residual effects of PTSD resulting from narcissistic abuse. Developing a toolkit of healthy strategies—such as mindfulness, journaling, and creative expression—can provide individuals with the resources needed to navigate challenging emotions. These practices promote self-awareness and emotional regulation, helping to mitigate feelings of anxiety and depression. Building resilience involves not only recognizing triggers but actively engaging in practices that nurture mental well-being and reinforce a sense of agency in one's life.

COPING WITH CHAOS

THE LINK BETWEEN NARCISSISM AND MENTAL HEALTH DISORDERS

Understanding Co-occurring Disorders

Understanding co-occurring disorders is essential for anyone navigating the aftermath of a relationship with a narcissist. Individuals who have experienced narcissistic abuse often find themselves grappling with a complex interplay of mental health challenges, including PTSD, depression, and anxiety. These disorders do not exist in isolation; rather, they intertwine, creating a web of emotional turmoil that can feel overwhelming. Recognizing how these conditions coexist is the first step toward healing, allowing for a more comprehensive approach to recovery. By understanding the interconnectedness of these issues, individuals can begin to dismantle the layers of pain and confusion that have accumulated over time.

The trauma bond formed in a relationship with a narcissist can significantly contribute to the development of co-occurring disorders. This bond, characterized by a cycle of manipulation and emotional dependency, can leave victims feeling trapped and powerless. As they seek to break free, the emotional fallout can manifest as PTSD, anxiety, and depressive symptoms. By acknowledging this bond and its impact on mental health, survivors can begin to untangle the emotional ties that bind them to their abuser. This understanding fosters resilience, empowering individuals to reclaim their autonomy and recognize that healing is not only possible but also a worthy pursuit.

Furthermore, the link between narcissism and mental health disorders is crucial to comprehend. Narcissistic abuse often inflicts deep psychological scars, resulting in symptoms that mirror those of PTSD. Survivors may experience flashbacks, hypervigilance, and an overwhelming sense of hopelessness. These symptoms can be exacerbated by co-occurring conditions, creating a cycle of despair that feels insurmountable. However, recognizing PTSD as an injury rather than a disorder can shift the narrative. By viewing trauma through the lens of injury, survivors can approach their healing with the understanding that it requires care, time, and a deliberate effort to address both the psychological and emotional wounds.

Embracing the concept of post-traumatic growth is vital for those recovering from narcissistic relationships. While the journey through trauma can be arduous, it can also lead to profound personal transformation. Understanding co-occurring disorders allows individuals to cultivate coping mechanisms that promote resilience and growth. By engaging in therapeutic practices, establishing support networks, and prioritizing self-care, survivors can navigate their healing journey with intention. This proactive approach not only addresses the symptoms of their co-occurring disorders but also paves the way for a future defined by strength and self-discovery.

Ultimately, identifying and overcoming suicidal ideation is a critical aspect of managing co-occurring disorders. The aftermath of narcissistic abuse can leave individuals feeling isolated and hopeless, intensifying thoughts of self-harm. However, by fostering a deeper understanding of their mental health, survivors can learn to recognize the warning signs and seek help. It is essential to create an environment where open dialogue about mental health is encouraged, allowing individuals to articulate their struggles without fear of stigma. With the right support and resources, healing becomes not just a possibility but a journey toward reclaiming one's life, filled with hope, purpose, and a renewed sense of self.

The Psychological Effects of Narcissism

The psychological effects of narcissism can be profound and far-reaching, particularly for those who have been subjected to its emotional toll. Individuals entangled in relationships with narcissists often experience a unique form of trauma that can lead to long-lasting psychological scars. The constant manipulation, gaslighting, and invalidation create a chaotic emotional environment, leaving victims feeling disoriented and questioning their own reality. This emotional drain can manifest in various ways, such as anxiety, depression, and in some cases, suicidal ideation. Understanding these effects is crucial for those seeking to heal and reclaim their lives.

1. One of the most significant psychological consequences of narcissistic abuse is the development of **trauma bonds**. These bonds form as victims become psychologically and emotionally tethered to their abuser, often leading to a cycle of hope and despair. The intermittent reinforcement of affection and attention from the narcissist can create a powerful psychological pull, making it difficult for individuals to break free from the toxic relationship. Recognizing this bond is the first step toward breaking the cycle and regaining autonomy. By understanding the nature of these bonds, individuals can begin to disentangle themselves from the emotional chaos and reclaim their sense of self.

2. Post-Traumatic Stress Disorder (PTSD) is often a direct result of enduring narcissistic abuse, yet it is essential to redefine our understanding of PTSD. Viewing it not merely as a disorder but as an injury that requires care and attention can empower survivors. This perspective encourages individuals to seek appropriate treatment and support, recognizing that healing from trauma is a journey that requires time and self-compassion.

By treating PTSD as an injury, survivors can focus on their recovery, actively engaging in therapeutic practices that foster healing and resilience.

3. Moreover, the aftermath of narcissistic relationships often includes a spectrum of mental health issues, including **depression and anxiety**. These conditions are not merely side effects; they are legitimate responses to the emotional abuse suffered. Acknowledging the link between narcissism and these mental health disorders can help victims understand that their feelings are valid and that healing is possible. By seeking professional help and employing coping mechanisms tailored to their experiences, individuals can begin to navigate the complexities of their emotional landscape and find a path toward recovery.

Ultimately, the journey toward post-traumatic growth is a testament to the resilience of the human spirit. Many individuals emerge from the shadows of narcissistic abuse with newfound strength, clarity, and purpose. By embracing this growth, survivors can transform their pain into a source of empowerment, fostering a deeper understanding of themselves and their needs. Through education, support, and self-care, it is possible to transcend the effects of narcissism and build a life filled with joy and fulfillment. Recovery is not just about surviving; it is about thriving, and the journey toward healing is one that can lead to a brighter, more hopeful future.

The journey of healing from narcissistic abuse is a testament to the resilience of the human spirit.

COPING MECHANISMS FOR PTSD

Healthy Coping Strategies

Healthy coping strategies are essential for anyone navigating the tumultuous aftermath of a relationship with a narcissist. These strategies not only facilitate healing but also empower individuals to redefine their lives beyond the shadow of trauma. By understanding that PTSD is an injury requiring care and not just a disorder, individuals can begin to approach their recovery with the same seriousness they would apply to a physical injury. This shift in perspective is crucial in fostering resilience and promoting a sense of agency over one's emotional well-being.

MINDFULNESS One effective coping strategy is the practice of mindfulness. Engaging in mindfulness allows individuals to ground themselves in the present moment, reducing the overwhelming feelings associated with anxiety and depression. Techniques such as deep breathing, meditation, or even simple observation of one's surroundings can help in calming the mind and body. By consistently incorporating these practices into daily life, individuals can create a sanctuary of peace that counters the chaos instilled by narcissistic abuse. This sanctuary becomes a vital tool in breaking the cycle of trauma bonds, enabling the individual to reclaim their identity and emotional autonomy.

SUPPORT NETWORK Connecting with others who have experienced similar traumas can foster understanding and validation. Support groups, therapy, and even close friendships provide a safe space for sharing experiences without judgment. This connection not only combats feelings of isolation but also reinforces the idea that healing is a communal journey. By leaning on others, individuals can draw strength from shared stories and gain insights into their own healing process, ultimately contributing to post-traumatic growth.

ENGAGING IN CREATIVE OUTLETS serves as another profound coping mechanism. Art, writing, music, or any form of self-expression can channel complex emotions into something tangible. This process not only aids in processing trauma but also fosters a sense of accomplishment and joy. Creativity allows individuals to explore their feelings deeply and can provide clarity and insight into their experiences. As they transform pain into art, they reclaim their narrative, empowering themselves to move forward toward a brighter future.

SETTING SMALL, ACHIEVABLE GOALS can help individuals cultivate a sense of purpose and direction. In the aftermath of narcissistic abuse, it's common to feel lost or directionless. By breaking down larger aspirations into manageable steps, individuals can celebrate small victories along the way. This practice encourages self-efficacy and reinforces the idea that recovery is a journey filled with progress, not perfection. Each step taken, no matter how small, is a testament to resilience and a powerful reminder that healing is not only possible but also within reach.

Mindfulness and Grounding Techniques

Mindfulness and grounding techniques serve as powerful tools for individuals grappling with the aftermath of narcissistic abuse. These practices encourage a return to the present moment, helping to dismantle the overwhelming feelings of anxiety and depression that often accompany PTSD. By focusing on the here and now, individuals can disrupt the cycle of negative thoughts and emotions that arise from trauma bonds, enabling a sense of safety and control. This shift in focus is essential for those seeking to reclaim their lives after the emotional turmoil inflicted by a narcissistic partner.

Practicing mindfulness involves cultivating an awareness of one's thoughts, feelings, and bodily sensations without judgment. Simple techniques such as deep breathing, meditation, and body scans can provide immediate relief from distressing emotions. For instance, when anxiety threatens to engulf you, taking a few moments to breathe deeply and intentionally can help anchor you in the present. This practice not only calms the mind but also fosters a deeper connection to the body, which is crucial for healing from trauma. By learning to observe rather than react, individuals empower themselves to navigate their emotional landscape with greater resilience.

Grounding techniques complement mindfulness by providing a practical way to reconnect with reality during moments of heightened distress. These methods can be as simple as focusing on the sensation of your feet on the ground or the texture of an object in your hand. Engaging the senses allows you to shift your focus from intrusive thoughts or memories of the past to the present moment, creating a buffer against anxiety and despair. Over time, these techniques can help fortify your emotional resilience, enabling you to face triggers with a newfound sense of strength and composure.

Incorporating mindfulness and grounding practices into daily routines fosters a sense of stability and self-compassion. Creating moments of stillness amid the chaos can be transformative, allowing for reflection and nurturing of the self. Journaling about your experiences or expressing gratitude for small victories can enhance this practice, enabling deeper healing and growth. As you witness your progress, it becomes clear that PTSD is not merely a disorder but an injury that deserves care, attention, and respect. This acknowledgment is a vital step toward embracing the journey of recovery and personal empowerment.

Mindfulness and grounding techniques pave the way for post-traumatic growth, encouraging individuals to thrive after the pain of narcissistic relationships. By developing these skills, you can break free from the shackles of trauma bonds and reclaim your narrative. Your journey, while challenging, is also an opportunity for profound transformation. Embracing these practices not only aids in the healing process but also cultivates a life filled with hope, purpose, and renewed strength. Through commitment to mindfulness and grounding, you can indeed navigate the path toward a brighter future, one day at a time.

Seeking Professional Help

Seeking professional help is a crucial step in the journey toward healing from the emotional and psychological wounds inflicted by narcissistic abuse. Many individuals grappling with PTSD and suicidal thoughts may feel overwhelmed, trapped in a cycle of despair that seems unbreakable. However, understanding that you are not alone in this struggle can provide a glimmer of hope. Professional support offers a safe space where you can express your feelings, explore your experiences, and begin to unravel the complex web of trauma bonds that may have formed during your relationship with a narcissist. Seeking help is not a sign of weakness; it is a courageous acknowledgment of your need for support and guidance.

Therapists and counselors trained in trauma-informed care can provide essential tools and strategies for managing the aftermath of emotional abuse. They can help you recognize the symptoms of PTSD and understand that it is an injury that requires treatment, much like a physical wound. This perspective shift is empowering, as it allows you to approach your healing process with the mindset that recovery is not only possible but also a journey of growth. Through therapy, you can learn coping mechanisms tailored to your unique experiences, allowing you to process your emotions and gradually regain control over your life.

The therapeutic relationship itself can be transformative. In a supportive environment, you can break free from the isolation that often accompanies trauma. As you share your story with someone who understands the nuances of narcissistic abuse, you may find validation and relief. This connection fosters trust, which is fundamental in healing. With the guidance of a professional, you can start to challenge the beliefs instilled by the narcissist, such as feelings of unworthiness, guilt, or shame. Through this process, you can reclaim your voice and redefine your identity, paving the way for post-traumatic growth.

In addition to traditional therapy, exploring support groups can also be beneficial. These spaces provide a community of individuals who have faced similar challenges, allowing you to share experiences and learn from one another. The power of collective healing cannot be underestimated; the understanding and empathy found in these groups can be a vital lifeline. As you connect with others who have experienced the devastating effects of narcissistic relationships, you will discover that healing is not a solitary journey. Together, you can inspire each other to take steps toward recovery and resilience.

Ultimately, seeking professional help signifies a commitment to your well-being and a desire to break the cycle of suffering. Remember that healing is a process that takes time, patience, and perseverance. By prioritizing your mental health and seeking the support you need, you are taking a monumental step toward reclaiming your life and thriving beyond the shadows of your past. Embrace this journey as an opportunity for growth, and trust that with each step forward, you are moving closer to a brighter, more fulfilling future.

The path to healing from narcissistic abuse is paved with self-compassion, self-care, and a commitment to personal growth. It is a journey of rediscovering your own strength and resilience.

The Importance of Validating Your Experience

Validating your experience is a crucial step in the journey of healing from the aftermath of narcissistic abuse. Many individuals grappling with the emotional fallout from such relationships often encounter self-doubt, feeling as if their experiences were not significant or worthy of acknowledgment. This mindset can be deeply damaging, as it not only trivializes the pain endured but also perpetuates feelings of isolation and despair. Recognizing the validity of your suffering is foundational; it paves the way for understanding the trauma you've faced, allowing you to move forward with a sense of purpose and empowerment.

Acknowledging the reality of your experiences can be transformative. When you validate your feelings and the impact of the abuse, you begin to dismantle the trauma bond that may still tether you to your abuser. This process involves recognizing that the emotional manipulation and control you endured were not just figments of your imagination but real experiences that have shaped your life. By confronting these truths, you can reclaim your narrative and shift the focus from guilt and shame to self-compassion and healing. Each acknowledgment serves as a step toward breaking free from the toxic patterns that have held you captive.

Understanding the importance of validating your experience also extends to recognizing PTSD as an injury rather than a mere disorder. This perspective allows you to treat your mental health with the same seriousness and care that you would apply to a physical injury. Just as a broken bone requires attention and rehabilitation, so too does the emotional trauma resulting from narcissistic abuse. By embracing this view, you empower yourself to seek the necessary support, whether through therapy, support groups, or self-care practices, and to treat your healing journey as a valid and essential endeavor.

As you navigate the complexities of recovery, it becomes essential to engage in practices that reinforce your validation. Journaling, speaking with trusted friends or professionals, and participating in support groups can facilitate a deeper understanding of your experiences. Sharing your story not only helps you articulate your pain but also connects you with others who have walked similar paths. This connection can foster a sense of belonging and understanding, reminding you that you are not alone in your struggle. Each step you take toward validation is a declaration of your strength and resilience.

Ultimately, validating your experience is a powerful act of self-love that can ignite post-traumatic growth. It opens doors to newfound perspectives and opportunities for thriving beyond the confines of past abuse. By recognizing your pain as legitimate, you set the stage for healing, growth, and a renewed sense of self. Embrace this journey with courage, knowing that every acknowledgment and act of validation brings you closer to the life you deserve—one filled with hope, healing, and the freedom to thrive beyond the shadows of narcissistic abuse.

Creating a Personal Recovery Plan

Creating a personal recovery plan is an empowering step in the journey toward healing from the emotional turmoil caused by narcissistic abuse. This plan serves as a roadmap, guiding you through the complexities of recovery while recognizing that PTSD is not merely a disorder but an injury that requires dedicated care and attention. Start by acknowledging your unique experiences and the challenges they have brought into your life. This is not just a checklist; it is a deeply personal commitment to yourself and your well-being. By embracing your narrative, you lay the foundation for your healing journey.

1. Begin by identifying your triggers and the situations that exacerbate your symptoms. Understanding what ignites feelings of anxiety, depression, or suicidal ideation is crucial in developing strategies to manage these responses. Create a list of your specific triggers, along with a plan to confront or avoid them when possible. This awareness transforms your experience from a passive reaction to an active engagement with your mental health, allowing you to reclaim some control over your life. Remember, recognizing triggers is not a sign of weakness; it is an essential aspect of self-empowerment and resilience.
2. Next, incorporate coping mechanisms that resonate with you. This may include mindfulness practices, journaling, or engaging in creative outlets that allow for self-expression. Physical activity can also be a powerful tool for recovery, as it not only boosts your mood but also helps release pent-up emotions. Experiment with different techniques and find what works best for you. By actively participating in your healing, you cultivate a sense of agency and hope, reinforcing the belief that recovery is not only possible but within your reach.
3. Building a support network is another vital component of your recovery plan. Surround yourself with individuals who understand your journey and can provide encouragement, empathy, and accountability. This could be friends, family members, or support groups specifically designed for survivors of narcissistic abuse. Sharing your experiences and connecting with others who have faced similar challenges can foster a sense of belonging and validation. Remember, you are not alone in this journey; there are many who have walked this path and emerged stronger.

4. Finally, set realistic and achievable goals for your recovery. These goals should encompass various aspects of your life, including emotional, physical, and social well-being. Celebrate small victories along the way, as they contribute to your overall progress. Each step you take toward healing is a testament to your resilience and strength. By actively engaging in your recovery plan, you redefine your relationship with PTSD and reclaim your life from the shadows of narcissistic abuse. Embrace the journey ahead, knowing that post-traumatic growth is not only achievable but a testament to your unwavering spirit.

Addressing Mental Health Challenges

Addressing mental health challenges after experiencing narcissistic abuse requires a multifaceted approach that prioritizes healing and growth. Understanding that PTSD is not merely a disorder but an injury that needs proper care is crucial. This perspective allows survivors to acknowledge their pain without judgment and to seek the necessary support. Embracing this mindset empowers individuals to view their experiences as a catalyst for change, fostering resilience and strength that can be harnessed in the recovery journey.

Breaking free from the trauma bond created by a relationship with a narcissist is often the first step toward healing. Recognizing the patterns of manipulation and emotional drain is essential for dismantling the hold that such relationships can have. It is vital to understand that recovery involves not just escaping the cycle of abuse but also redefining one's identity outside of that relationship. This process may include seeking therapy, engaging in supportive communities, and practicing self-compassion, which collectively lay the groundwork for reclaiming one's life.

Coping mechanisms play a critical role in managing PTSD, depression, and anxiety resulting from emotional abuse. Survivors can benefit from a range of strategies, including mindfulness practices, journaling, and physical activities that promote well-being. Establishing a routine that incorporates these activities can provide a sense of normalcy and help individuals regain control over their lives. Additionally, seeking professional help can be invaluable in developing personalized coping strategies that address specific triggers and symptoms, fostering a sense of empowerment and agency.

Addressing suicidal ideation is a crucial aspect of the healing journey. It is essential to recognize that these thoughts are often a response to overwhelming pain and hopelessness. Creating a safety plan, reaching out to trusted friends or professionals, and engaging in crisis intervention resources can provide immediate support in times of crisis. By openly discussing these feelings and seeking help, survivors can find a path toward healing, ultimately redefining their relationship with themselves and building a future filled with hope and possibility.

EMOTIONAL INTELLIGENCE AND RELATIONSHIPS

The Importance of Emotional Intelligence

Emotional intelligence is a cornerstone for fostering healthy and positive relationships, especially for those navigating the turbulent waters of narcissistic abuse. In the context of recovery, emotional intelligence equips individuals with the skills necessary to recognize their own emotions and understand the feelings of others. This heightened awareness can act as a protective barrier against the manipulative tactics often employed by narcissists. By cultivating emotional intelligence, survivors can gain clarity in their interactions, making it easier to identify red flags and disengage from toxic dynamics before they cause further harm.

The journey of healing from narcissistic abuse is deeply intertwined with the development of emotional intelligence. Survivors often face a barrage of conflicting emotions, from anger and betrayal to confusion and fear. Learning to regulate these emotions is essential for personal growth and recovery. Techniques such as mindfulness, reflective journaling, and supportive therapy can enhance emotional awareness, allowing individuals to process their trauma in healthier ways. This internal work not only aids in recovery but also empowers victims to reclaim their narratives and step into their authenticity.

In understanding narcissistic personality disorder, emotional intelligence plays a vital role in distinguishing between the disorder as an inherent condition and narcissism as a learned behavior. Individuals equipped with strong emotional intelligence can approach these interactions with empathy while also maintaining necessary boundaries. This balance is crucial; it enables the individual to respond rather than react, fostering a sense of control that is often stripped away in toxic relationships. By recognizing that narcissism can manifest in both tendencies and choices, survivors can better navigate their relationships and understand the patterns at play.

Building emotional intelligence is not merely a tool for survival; it is a pathway to empowerment. Strategies such as active listening, empathy exercises, and emotional regulation techniques can transform one's ability to engage in meaningful connections. As individuals learn to articulate their feelings and needs, they also cultivate healthier relationships with themselves and others. This process of growth not only enhances personal resilience but also contributes to a broader understanding of emotional health, fostering a community of support among those who have experienced similar traumas.

The importance of emotional intelligence in the context of toxic relationships cannot be overstated. It serves as both a shield and a sword, protecting individuals from further harm while also equipping them with the tools to thrive. By embracing emotional intelligence, survivors of narcissistic abuse can break free from the cycle of trauma and forge new paths towards healing and fulfillment. In doing so, they not only reclaim their own lives but also inspire others to seek the emotional growth needed to navigate their own journeys of recovery.

Building Emotional Intelligence: Strategies for Personal Growth

Building emotional intelligence is a crucial strategy for personal growth, especially for those who have experienced the turmoil of toxic relationships. Emotional intelligence, the ability to recognize, understand, and manage our own emotions while also empathizing with others, empowers individuals to navigate the complexities of their feelings and interactions. For survivors of narcissistic abuse, cultivating emotional intelligence can be a transformative journey, allowing them to reclaim their sense of self and build healthier relationships. By embracing this journey, individuals can break free from the shadows of their past and foster a brighter, more connected future.

1. One effective strategy for enhancing emotional intelligence is self-awareness. This involves taking the time to reflect on one's emotions, thoughts, and behaviors. Journaling can be a powerful tool, providing a safe space to articulate and explore feelings that may have been suppressed during toxic

relationships. By identifying triggers and patterns, individuals can gain insight into their emotional responses and develop a deeper understanding of how their experiences shape their reactions. This self-reflection not only builds emotional intelligence but also nurtures resilience, which is vital in the healing process.

2. Another vital component of emotional intelligence is empathy. Developing the ability to understand and share the feelings of others fosters deeper connections and promotes healthier interactions. Practicing active listening—truly hearing what others say without planning a response—can enhance empathy. This skill allows individuals to validate the feelings of others, creating an environment of trust and support. For those recovering from narcissistic abuse, learning to empathize with others can also be a way to redefine relationships on a healthier foundation, breaking away from the isolation often felt in toxic dynamics.

3. Emotion regulation is equally essential in building emotional intelligence. Survivors of narcissistic relationships often experience intense emotional responses, which can be overwhelming. Implementing techniques such as mindfulness and deep-breathing exercises can help manage these responses. Mindfulness encourages individuals to stay present, reducing the anxiety that can stem from past trauma. By practicing emotional regulation, individuals can respond to challenges with clarity rather than reacting impulsively, ultimately fostering a sense of control over their emotional landscape.

4. Lastly, seeking support from others is an invaluable strategy for building emotional intelligence. Engaging with support groups or therapy can provide a safe space to share experiences and gain new perspectives. Surrounding oneself

with understanding individuals who validate one's journey can enhance emotional growth. Through connection and shared experiences, individuals can learn from each other, discover new coping mechanisms, and empower one another in their healing journeys. In embracing these strategies, individuals can cultivate a robust emotional intelligence that not only aids in recovery from narcissistic abuse but also serves as a foundation for cultivating healthier, more fulfilling relationships in the future.

NAVIGATING TOXIC RELATIONSHIPS

Identifying Red Flags

Identifying red flags in relationships is crucial for anyone seeking to protect themselves from the insidious effects of narcissistic abuse. These warning signs often manifest subtly at first, making them easy to overlook. However, being aware of these indicators can empower individuals to make informed decisions about their relationships and prioritize their emotional well-being. A consistent pattern of self-centered behavior, manipulation, and emotional volatility can serve as a foundation for recognizing a toxic dynamic before it spirals into deeper pain.

LACK OF EMPATHY One of the most prominent red flags is a lack of empathy. Narcissists often struggle to understand or care about the feelings of others, which can lead to dismissive or hurtful behavior. When someone consistently invalidates your emotions or prioritizes their own needs over yours, it's a signal that the relationship may be toxic. This emotional neglect can erode self-esteem and create an environment of confusion and self-doubt, trapping victims in a cycle of seeking validation from their abuser while feeling increasingly isolated.

PRESENCE OF MANIPULATION AND CONTROL

Another critical indicator is the presence of manipulation and control. Narcissists tend to employ tactics such as gaslighting, where they distort reality to undermine your confidence and perceptions. If you frequently find yourself questioning your own thoughts or feelings because of someone else's insistence that you are wrong, this is a significant red flag. Recognizing these manipulative behaviors can be the first step towards reclaiming your truth and breaking free from the psychological grip of a narcissist.

PATTERNS OF LOVE-BOMBING FOLLOWED BY WITHDRAWAL

Additionally, watch for patterns of love-bombing followed by withdrawal. Initially, a narcissist may shower you with affection and attention, creating an intoxicating sense of connection. However, this can quickly turn into emotional distance and criticism, leaving you feeling unworthy and desperate for their approval. This push-and-pull dynamic can be incredibly damaging, fostering a sense of dependency that keeps you trapped in the toxic cycle. Acknowledging this pattern allows you to step back and assess the health of the relationship critically.

Ultimately, identifying red flags is not just about recognizing harmful behaviors; it is about cultivating emotional intelligence and fostering resilience. By learning to trust your instincts and set healthy boundaries, you can protect yourself from the emotional turmoil that often accompanies toxic relationships. Education and awareness are vital tools in this journey, empowering you to make choices that prioritize your emotional health and well-being. Healing from narcissistic abuse is possible, and understanding these warning signs is a pivotal step toward reclaiming your life and building healthier, more fulfilling relationships.

Coping Mechanisms for Survivors

Survivors of narcissistic abuse often find themselves navigating a tumultuous emotional landscape, marked by confusion, self-doubt, and lingering trauma. To reclaim their sense of self, it is vital for these individuals to adopt effective coping mechanisms that facilitate healing and personal growth. One of the most empowering strategies involves building a robust support system. Engaging with trusted friends, family members, or support groups can provide a safe space to share experiences and foster understanding. This connection helps counteract feelings of isolation and reinforces the knowledge that survivors are not alone in their journey toward recovery.

1. Another essential coping mechanism is the practice of mindfulness and self-compassion. Mindfulness encourages individuals to remain present and acknowledge their feelings without judgment. This approach can be transformative, allowing survivors to recognize and validate their emotions. By incorporating self-compassion into their routines, survivors can cultivate a nurturing inner dialogue, replacing self-criticism with kindness. Techniques such as meditation, journaling, or simply taking time to reflect can help individuals reconnect with their inner selves and foster a sense of peace amidst the chaos of their past experiences.
2. Emotional regulation plays a critical role in managing the trauma responses that often accompany narcissistic abuse. Survivors can benefit from learning specific tools aimed at regulating their emotions, such as deep breathing exercises, grounding techniques, or visualization practices. These strategies empower individuals to regain control over their emotional state, reducing anxiety and enhancing resilience. By developing a toolkit of emotional regulation strategies, survivors

can navigate triggers more effectively and create a sense of stability in their daily lives.

3. In addition to emotional regulation, establishing healthy boundaries is vital for survivors as they rebuild their lives. Learning to assertively communicate needs and limits not only protects their well-being but also fosters a sense of agency. This practice requires self-awareness and courage but ultimately allows survivors to reclaim their power, reinforcing their commitment to self-care and personal growth. By surrounding themselves with positive influences and distancing from toxic interactions, survivors can create a nurturing environment that supports their healing journey.

Ultimately, the path to recovery from narcissistic abuse is a deeply personal and transformative process. By embracing coping mechanisms such as building support systems, practicing mindfulness, regulating emotions, and establishing healthy boundaries, survivors can embark on a journey toward empowerment and healing. Each step taken in this direction reinforces their resilience and capacity for growth, illuminating the strength that lies within. As survivors continue to unveil the truth behind their experiences, they pave the way for a brighter future, one where they can thrive and cultivate fulfilling relationships based on mutual respect and emotional intelligence.

Support Systems for Victims

Support systems for victims of narcissistic abuse are essential in the journey toward healing and recovery. These systems can take various forms, including friends, family, support groups, and professional therapists. Each plays a crucial role in helping individuals regain their sense of self and navigate the complexities of their emotional landscape.

It is vital for victims to recognize that they are not alone in their struggles, and there are people and resources available to support them through this challenging journey.

Friends and family can often provide the initial layer of support, offering a safe space where victims can share their experiences without fear of judgment. However, it is important for these loved ones to educate themselves about narcissistic abuse to truly understand the emotional turmoil their friend or family member is facing. This understanding fosters empathy and allows them to offer informed support. Encouraging open conversations around feelings and experiences can help victims feel validated and understood, which is a significant step in rebuilding their shattered self-esteem.

In addition to informal support, professional help is a cornerstone of recovery. Therapists specializing in trauma and narcissistic abuse can equip victims with the tools necessary to process their experiences and rebuild their lives. Therapy not only provides a safe environment to explore painful emotions but also introduces coping strategies and techniques for emotional regulation. Groups focused on narcissistic abuse recovery can provide a unique sense of community, where individuals can connect with others who have faced similar challenges. This shared understanding can cultivate a powerful sense of belonging and lessen feelings of isolation.

Support systems also play a vital role in empowering victims to reclaim their narratives. Education about narcissistic personality disorder and its effects can demystify the experiences of abuse, helping victims understand that the behaviors of their abuser were not a reflection of their worth. This empowerment through knowledge encourages individuals to set boundaries and recognize red flags in future relationships, fostering healthier dynamics. Furthermore, developing emotional intelligence through workshops and self-help resources can enhance personal growth, enabling survivors to build more fulfilling and resilient connections.

Ultimately, the path to healing from narcissistic abuse is not a solitary endeavor. Support systems provide the crucial framework needed for victims to feel safe, understood, and empowered. By fostering connections with empathetic individuals and professionals, victims can navigate their trauma with greater resilience and strength. The journey may be difficult, but with the right support, it is possible to emerge from the shadows of abuse, reclaim one's identity, and cultivate a life filled with joy, authenticity, and healthy relationships.

NARCISSISM AND MENTAL HEALTH

The Link Between Narcissism and Anxiety

The intricate relationship between narcissism and anxiety reveals a complex interplay that can significantly affect individuals on both ends of the spectrum. Narcissists often present a facade of confidence and self-assuredness, yet beneath this outward appearance lies a profound vulnerability. This vulnerability can lead to heightened anxiety, particularly when their self-image is threatened. The fear of inadequacy drives many narcissists to engage in behaviors that may seem grandiose, but these are often compensatory mechanisms to mask their deep-seated insecurities. Understanding this connection is crucial for both those who identify narcissistic traits in themselves and those navigating relationships with narcissistic individuals.

Anxiety manifests in narcissistic individuals in various ways. For some, it may lead to defensive behaviors aimed at preserving their self-image, resulting in emotional manipulation and control over their surroundings. Conversely, vulnerable narcissists often experience anxiety more acutely, struggling with feelings of inferiority and self-doubt. This form of narcissism is characterized by a deep need for validation, making them particularly sensitive to criticism. The constant need to seek approval can create a cycle of anxiety, as external validation becomes a lifeline, perpetuating their emotional turmoil. Recognizing these patterns serves as a vital step toward understanding the broader implications of narcissism.

In romantic relationships, the link between narcissism and anxiety can be especially detrimental. Partners of narcissists may find themselves caught in a web of emotional highs and lows, often feeling anxious due to the unpredictable nature of their partner's behavior. This dynamic can create a toxic environment where the narcissist's anxiety spills over, leading to emotional manipulation and control. Understanding how anxiety drives narcissistic behavior can empower individuals to set healthier boundaries and foster emotional resilience. By acknowledging these patterns, partners can take proactive steps to protect their mental health and well-being.

The workplace also provides fertile ground for the interplay between narcissism and anxiety. Narcissistic leaders may exhibit a commanding presence, yet their underlying anxiety can lead to erratic decision-making and a lack of empathy for their colleagues. Employees may experience heightened stress levels as they navigate the demands of a narcissistic boss, who may project their anxiety onto others. Recognizing these traits can help individuals develop strategies for coping and establishing a supportive work environment. By fostering open communication and promoting mental well-being, workplaces can mitigate the impact of narcissism and anxiety on overall morale.

Ultimately, understanding the link between narcissism and anxiety is a pathway toward healing and growth. It empowers individuals to recognize the traits in themselves and others, fostering a deeper understanding of emotional dynamics in various relationships. By acknowledging these connections, individuals can cultivate healthier interactions, whether in romantic partnerships, friendships, or professional settings. This profound understanding of narcissism not only aids in personal development but also equips individuals to navigate the complexities of their relationships with greater confidence and emotional clarity.

Narcissism and Depression

Narcissism and depression are intricately linked, revealing a complex interplay that shapes the emotional landscape of individuals affected by these traits. While narcissism is often characterized by self-importance, a need for admiration, and a lack of empathy, those who exhibit vulnerable narcissism frequently grapple with feelings of inadequacy and deep-seated insecurity. This paradox highlights how beneath the facade of confidence and entitlement, many narcissists may experience profound emotional turmoil, leading to symptoms of depression. Understanding this connection is essential for recognizing the signs of narcissism and its impact on mental health.

Individuals with narcissistic traits often employ defense mechanisms to shield themselves from feelings of worthlessness, yet these strategies can lead to a cycle of isolation and despair. When faced with criticism or rejection, a narcissist may react with anger or contempt, but internally, they may plunge into feelings of sadness and hopelessness. This emotional volatility can strain relationships and create a toxic environment, both for the narcissist and those around them. Recognizing these patterns is crucial for anyone navigating a relationship with a narcissist, as it can provide insight into their behavior and its underlying motivations.

The types of narcissism—grandiose and vulnerable—further illuminate this connection between narcissism and depression. Grandiose narcissists may appear confident and successful, but their self-image often relies heavily on external validation. When that validation falters, they may encounter depressive symptoms masked by arrogance. Vulnerable narcissists, on the other hand, are more likely to experience overt depression due to their heightened sensitivity to rejection and perceived slights. Understanding these distinctions enables individuals to better empathize with the struggles of those who display narcissistic traits, fostering a more profound comprehension of their behaviors and emotional experiences.

Cultural influences also play a significant role in shaping narcissistic traits and their correlation with depression. In societies that emphasize individualism and success, the pressure to maintain a flawless self-image can exacerbate feelings of inadequacy and despair among narcissists. This cultural backdrop creates a breeding ground for emotional manipulation and unhealthy relationships, as narcissists may struggle to reconcile their self-perception with societal expectations. By examining these cultural dynamics, we can better understand how narcissism manifests and the potential for depression within different contexts.

Healing after a relationship with a narcissist often involves addressing the emotional scars left by their behavior. Individuals who have been affected by narcissism can benefit from therapeutic strategies that focus on rebuilding self-esteem, fostering self-compassion, and developing healthier relationship patterns. Recognizing the signs of narcissism and its impact on mental health is the first step toward recovery. By cultivating awareness and understanding, it becomes possible to break free from the cycle of manipulation and emotional distress, paving the way for a more fulfilling and authentic life.

Treatment Approaches

Treatment approaches for individuals affected by narcissism, whether as individuals exhibiting narcissistic traits or those impacted by such personalities, require a nuanced understanding of the spectrum of narcissism. Therapeutic interventions can vary significantly, but they generally focus on fostering self-awareness, empathy, and healthier relational dynamics. Cognitive behavioral therapy (CBT) is often effective, as it helps individuals recognize distorted thought patterns and encourages the development of healthier coping mechanisms. This method allows those with narcissistic tendencies to explore the roots of their behavior and understand how it affects their relationships, paving the way for personal growth and transformation.

For those entangled in relationships with narcissists, whether romantic or familial, it is crucial to establish boundaries and prioritize self-care. Therapeutic support, such as individual counseling or support groups, can be invaluable in helping individuals process their experiences and reclaim their sense of self. These safe spaces encourage sharing and validation, which are essential for healing from emotional manipulation and the psychological toll that often accompanies narcissistic dynamics. Empowerment through education about narcissism and its effects can also fortify individuals, enabling them to make informed decisions about their relationships.

In the context of parenting a narcissist, approaches can be particularly challenging, as these relationships often involve deep emotional entanglement. Parent-focused therapy can assist in developing strategies for setting boundaries while maintaining a sense of personal identity. It's important for these parents to cultivate self-compassion and seek support from professionals who understand the nuances of narcissistic behavior. This supportive framework can help mitigate the emotional distress that arises from such interactions and provide a pathway toward healthier family dynamics.

Ultimately, the path to healing from narcissism—whether as an individual exhibiting these traits or as someone recovering from a relationship with a narcissist—requires patience, commitment, and support. The journey may be fraught with challenges, but it is also filled with opportunities for profound personal growth and transformation. By embracing therapeutic strategies, fostering self-awareness, and cultivating empathy towards oneself and others, individuals can transcend the limitations imposed by narcissistic dynamics, paving the way for healthier, more fulfilling relationships in all aspects of life.

CULTURAL INFLUENCES ON NARCISSISM

Societal Trends and Narcissism

Societal trends play a pivotal role in shaping individual behaviors and personality traits, including narcissism. In recent years, we have witnessed a surge in social media usage, where curated identities and the pursuit of validation through likes and shares have become commonplace. This environment fosters a culture that often rewards self-promotion and superficial connections, contributing to an increase in narcissistic traits among individuals. As we navigate this landscape, it becomes essential to understand how these trends not only reflect but also amplify the characteristics of narcissism, leading to a society increasingly focused on image rather than substance.

Recognizing the main traits that all narcissists share is crucial in understanding their impact on relationships and social dynamics.

Narcissists often exhibit a lack of empathy, an inflated sense of self-importance, and an obsession with admiration. These traits are magnified in a society that celebrates individual achievement and personal branding, creating a fertile ground for narcissistic behavior. As adults, we must learn to identify these commonalities, allowing us to discern between healthy self-esteem and the harmful tendencies associated with narcissism. This awareness empowers us to set boundaries and protect ourselves in interactions with narcissistic individuals.

The types of narcissists vary, ranging from the overtly grandiose to the more vulnerable and insecure. Each type manifests narcissistic traits in different ways, influenced by societal factors and personal experiences. Understanding these distinctions is essential for navigating relationships, whether in romantic contexts, the workplace, or even within family dynamics. Recognizing that not all narcissists fit a single mold allows for a deeper comprehension of their behaviors and motivations, ultimately informing our approach to managing our interactions with them.

Cultural influences undeniably shape how narcissism is expressed and perceived. In a society that often equates success with visibility and self-promotion, individuals may feel pressured to adopt narcissistic traits to thrive. This cultural backdrop not only affects personal relationships but also impacts mental health, as individuals grapple with feelings of inadequacy when comparing themselves to the seemingly perfect lives portrayed online. Understanding these influences provides a framework for addressing and mitigating the negative effects of narcissism, both within ourselves and in our communities.

Healing from relationships with narcissistic individuals is a journey fraught with challenges, yet it is also an opportunity for profound personal growth. By recognizing the traits and behaviors of narcissists, we can develop strategies to safeguard our emotional well-being and rebuild our sense of self. Engaging with supportive communities, seeking professional guidance, and practicing self-compassion are vital steps in this process. As we emerge from the shadows of narcissistic relationships, we can cultivate resilience and foster healthier connections, ultimately contributing to a more empathetic and understanding society.

The Role of Social Media

The advent of social media has fundamentally transformed interpersonal dynamics, offering a unique platform for self-expression and connection. However, it has also created fertile ground for narcissistic behaviors to flourish. The instant gratification provided by likes, shares, and comments reinforces a self-centered worldview that many narcissists thrive on. By curating their online personas, they often present an idealized version of themselves, seeking validation and admiration from a vast audience. This constant craving for attention not only perpetuates their narcissistic traits but also influences how they interact with others in both virtual and real-life settings.

In the realm of romantic relationships, social media can serve as both a tool for connection and a breeding ground for manipulation. Narcissistic individuals may leverage social platforms to maintain control over their partners, using tactics such as monitoring online activity or creating jealousy through selective sharing. This behavior can lead to emotional turmoil for those involved, as the lines between reality and the curated online image blur. Understanding these dynamics is crucial for recognizing red flags and protecting oneself from the emotional fallout that often accompanies a relationship with a narcissist.

Moreover, the workplace is not immune to the impact of social media on narcissistic behaviors. Professionals may use platforms to showcase their achievements, often exaggerating their contributions or downplaying the efforts of colleagues. This competitive spirit can create a toxic environment where collaboration is stifled, and genuine connections are overshadowed by the need to outshine others. As employees navigate these challenging dynamics, it becomes essential to foster awareness and cultivate a culture that values authenticity over superficial accolades.

Parenting a narcissistic individual poses its challenges, especially in a world where social media can amplify their tendencies. Children raised in such environments may learn to equate self-worth with external validation, potentially perpetuating a cycle of narcissistic traits in future generations. Educating parents about the nuances of narcissism and its implications on child development is vital. Equipping them with strategies to promote healthy self-esteem and emotional intelligence can break this cycle and nurture resilience in their children.

Cultural influences further complicate the landscape of narcissism in the age of social media. In societies that prioritize individualism and self-promotion, narcissistic traits may be more readily accepted or even celebrated. Recognizing this cultural backdrop is essential for understanding the broader implications of narcissism and its impact on mental health and relationships. By fostering a collective awareness of these influences, individuals can better navigate their own experiences and cultivate healthier connections, both online and offline. Ultimately, embracing authenticity and empathy in the face of rising narcissism can lead to profound healing and growth for all involved.

Cultural Variations in Narcissistic Traits

Cultural variations in narcissistic traits reveal the complex interplay between individual behaviors and broader societal values. Different cultures shape the expression of narcissism, influencing how individuals perceive themselves and their relationships with others. In collectivist societies, where community and familial ties are prioritized, narcissistic traits may manifest differently than in individualistic cultures, where personal achievement and self-promotion are celebrated. Recognizing these differences is crucial for understanding the spectrum of narcissism and its impact on interpersonal dynamics.

In individualistic cultures, such as those found in many Western nations, narcissism often aligns with traits like self-assertion, entitlement, and a strong focus on personal success. Individuals may openly display their achievements and seek admiration, reflecting cultural norms that reward self-promotion. In contrast, in collectivist societies, narcissistic traits might be expressed through a veneer of humility, where individuals may seek validation through their contributions to the group rather than through personal accolades. This divergence highlights the importance of context in evaluating narcissistic behaviors and their implications for relationships.

Additionally, cultural narratives surrounding success and failure play a significant role in shaping narcissistic traits. In cultures that emphasize competition and individual triumph, individuals may develop grandiose self-perceptions, leading to a prevalence of overt narcissism. Conversely, in environments where cooperation and harmony are valued, narcissism may be more covert, with individuals displaying vulnerable traits marked by insecurity and a deep need for acceptance. This understanding allows for a more nuanced view of narcissism that takes into account the cultural lens through which behavior is interpreted.

The implications of these cultural variations extend into various domains, including romantic relationships, workplace dynamics, and parenting styles. In romantic contexts, the expectations and expressions of love and admiration can differ dramatically based on cultural backgrounds, affecting how narcissistic traits manifest and are tolerated. Similarly, in the workplace, cultural attitudes towards hierarchy and authority can influence the acceptance of narcissistic behaviors, shaping team interactions and leadership styles. Understanding these cultural nuances is essential for navigating relationships with narcissistic individuals effectively.

As we explore the spectrum of narcissism, recognizing these cultural influences empowers individuals to foster healthier relationships and develop strategies for healing. By understanding how cultural factors shape narcissistic traits, we can better identify and address these behaviors in our lives and the lives of those around us. This knowledge not only aids in personal growth but also enhances our ability to create supportive environments that discourage narcissistic tendencies, promoting empathy and connection across diverse cultural landscapes

NAVIGATING NARCISSISM IN THE WORKPLACE

Identifying Narcissistic Colleagues

Identifying narcissistic colleagues can be a challenging yet essential skill in fostering a healthy workplace. The nuances of narcissism range from overtly grandiose behaviors to more subtle, vulnerable expressions. The key lies in recognizing common traits shared by narcissists, such as a constant need for admiration, a lack of empathy, and manipulative tendencies. When these traits manifest in colleagues, they can create a toxic environment that stifles collaboration and undermines team cohesion. By understanding these characteristics, you can better navigate your professional relationships and protect your mental well-being.

One of the most telling signs of a narcissistic colleague is their overwhelming need for validation. They often dominate conversations, steering discussions toward their achievements while showing little interest in others' contributions. This self-centered behavior can be disheartening for team members who seek collaboration and mutual respect. Additionally, narcissistic individuals may engage in gaslighting, making colleagues doubt their perceptions and feelings. Recognizing these tactics early can help you maintain your confidence and assertiveness in a challenging work environment.

The workplace can reveal several types of narcissism, each with distinct traits and behaviors. While grandiose narcissists are easily identifiable due to their bold self-promotion and disregard for others, vulnerable narcissists may present as insecure, seeking attention through victimhood. Both types can significantly impact workplace dynamics. Understanding these distinctions allows you to anticipate potential conflicts and devise strategies to manage interactions effectively. By identifying the type of narcissism at play, you can tailor your approach to minimize their influence on your work life.

Cultural influences also play a significant role in shaping narcissistic behavior. Societies that prioritize individual achievement and status can foster narcissistic traits, making it crucial to recognize the broader context in which these behaviors occur. This understanding not only aids in identifying narcissistic colleagues but also encourages compassion for individuals who may be struggling with deep-seated insecurities. By fostering a more empathetic perspective, you can create a more supportive workplace environment while protecting yourself from the negative impact of narcissism.

Ultimately, identifying narcissistic colleagues allows you to establish boundaries and prioritize your emotional health. Recognizing the traits and behaviors associated with narcissism equips you with the tools needed to navigate challenging relationships with confidence. While it may be tempting to engage with narcissists in an attempt to change their behavior, often the most effective strategy is to maintain distance and focus on your own growth. By doing so, you can cultivate a thriving professional life that is free from the detrimental effects of narcissism.

Coping Strategies for Employees

In navigating the complex dynamics of a workplace influenced by narcissistic behaviors, employees can cultivate resilience through various coping strategies. Recognizing the traits of narcissism is the first step toward empowerment. Understanding whether a colleague exhibits grandiose or vulnerable narcissistic tendencies allows employees to tailor their responses effectively. By fostering awareness of these traits, individuals can prepare themselves mentally and emotionally, reducing the impact of narcissistic interactions on their well-being.

Setting clear boundaries is vital in maintaining a healthy work environment. Employees should feel empowered to assert themselves and prioritize their needs, even in the face of manipulative behaviors. Establishing limits on acceptable behavior can mitigate the stress and confusion often caused by narcissistic individuals. This proactive stance not only protects personal space but also promotes a culture of respect and accountability within the team.

Building a robust support network is another essential strategy. Engaging with colleagues who share similar experiences can provide validation and a sense of community. Sharing insights and strategies for coping with narcissistic behaviors fosters resilience and encourages collective strength. This camaraderie can help employees feel less isolated in their struggles, reinforcing the idea that they are not alone in facing these challenges.

Practicing self-care is crucial for employees dealing with narcissistic dynamics. Prioritizing physical and mental health through regular exercise, mindfulness practices, and hobbies allows individuals to recharge and maintain a balanced perspective. When employees invest time in self-care, they enhance their emotional resilience, enabling them to respond to workplace challenges with clarity and strength. This commitment to personal well-being can create a buffer against the negative effects of narcissism.

Finally, seeking professional guidance can be instrumental in navigating the complexities of working with narcissistic individuals. Therapy or coaching can provide invaluable tools for understanding interactions and developing effective coping mechanisms. Such support empowers employees to not only endure but thrive in challenging environments, transforming potential adversities into opportunities for personal growth and professional development. By embracing these coping strategies, employees can reclaim their power and foster a more harmonious workplace, ultimately leading to greater job satisfaction and fulfillment.

Leading with Empathy

Empathy serves as a powerful antidote to the divisive nature of narcissism. It allows individuals to connect on a deeper level, fostering understanding and compassion even in the face of challenging behaviors. In navigating relationships with narcissists, whether in romantic partnerships, workplaces, or familial structures, cultivating empathy can transform interactions. By recognizing the underlying pain and insecurities that often drive narcissistic tendencies, one can establish boundaries while still maintaining a sense of humanity in difficult situations. This approach not only aids in personal healing but also creates an environment where constructive dialogue can flourish.

Understanding the spectrum of narcissism requires a nuanced perspective that incorporates empathy. Each type, whether grandiose or vulnerable, reveals layers of emotional complexity. Those who exhibit grandiose traits may present themselves with an air of superiority, often masking deep-seated fears of inadequacy. Conversely, vulnerable narcissists may oscillate between self-pity and self-importance. Leading with empathy allows us to see beyond these defenses, recognizing the common human struggles that bind us all. By fostering an empathetic understanding, we can develop more effective strategies for engaging with narcissistic behavior while protecting our own emotional well-being.

In romantic relationships, empathy can act as a bridge to healthier dynamics. It encourages open communication and deeper emotional connections, even when faced with manipulative tendencies. By approaching discussions with a mindset rooted in empathy, partners can express their feelings without escalating conflicts. This emotional intelligence not only promotes mutual understanding but also empowers individuals to reclaim their narratives, breaking the cycle of emotional manipulation that often characterizes such relationships. When empathy is at the forefront, it becomes easier to identify unhealthy patterns while still honoring the shared humanity that exists between partners.

The workplace is another arena where empathy can profoundly impact interactions with narcissistic colleagues. Leading with empathy fosters a culture of respect and collaboration, disarming the often defensive and competitive nature of narcissistic personalities. When team members approach one another with compassion, they create an atmosphere where ideas can be exchanged freely, and individual contributions are valued. This shift not only enhances productivity but also mitigates the toxic effects of narcissism, allowing everyone to thrive. By prioritizing empathy, organizations can cultivate resilience, creating a workplace that champions emotional well-being alongside professional achievement.

Ultimately, leading with empathy is not merely a strategy for managing narcissistic relationships; it is a pathway toward personal growth and emotional healing. It challenges us to reflect on our own vulnerabilities and recognize the shared human experience. By embracing empathy, we cultivate resilience and foster a deeper sense of connection with ourselves and others, empowering us to navigate the complexities of narcissism with strength and grace. Through this journey, we not only enhance our relationships but also contribute to a more compassionate world, where understanding and empathy reign over division and isolation.

THE IMPACT OF NARCISSISM ON FAMILY DYNAMICS

Family Relationships and Narcissism

Family relationships profoundly shape our emotional landscape, and when narcissism enters the equation, the dynamics can shift dramatically. In families with a narcissistic member, there is often a pervasive sense of imbalance, where the needs and feelings of the narcissist overshadow those of others. This creates an environment where self-worth is contingent upon pleasing the narcissist, leading to feelings of inadequacy, shame, and confusion among family members. Recognizing the signs of narcissism within familial relationships is crucial for understanding the impact it has on emotional health and overall well-being.

The effects of growing up in a narcissistic family can be long-lasting and often manifest as emotional trauma. Children raised in such environments may struggle with self-esteem issues, anxiety, and a distorted sense of identity. They often learn to suppress their feelings, internalizing the belief that their emotions are invalid or unworthy. This emotional neglect can hinder their ability to form healthy, trusting relationships in adulthood. Healing from this trauma is not just about acknowledging the pain but also about reclaiming one's narrative and recognizing the inherent worth and value that each individual possesses.

Emotional intelligence plays a pivotal role in navigating the complexities of family relationships marked by narcissism. By developing the skills to understand and manage one's emotions, individuals can create a buffer against the toxic dynamics often present in these relationships. This involves recognizing narcissistic behaviors and understanding their impact while also fostering empathy and compassion for oneself. When emotional intelligence is cultivated, it empowers individuals to set healthy boundaries and communicate effectively, paving the way for healing and growth.

Identifying the red flags of narcissism within family dynamics is an essential step toward breaking free from the cycle of emotional abuse. Patterns such as manipulation, gaslighting, and emotional invalidation serve as indicators of a toxic environment that can stifle personal development. By becoming aware of these patterns, individuals can begin to detach themselves emotionally and seek healthier connections. It's important to remember that breaking away from these dynamics can be challenging, but it is a crucial step toward reclaiming one's life and fostering positive relationships.

Support systems are fundamental for those recovering from narcissistic abuse. Building a network of understanding friends, family, or support groups can provide the necessary encouragement and validation during the healing process. Empowerment through education is equally vital; understanding narcissism and its effects can help individuals recognize their experiences and feel less isolated. By sharing knowledge and experiences, survivors can cultivate resilience and inspire others, transforming their pain into a source of strength and hope for a brighter future.

Breaking the Cycle: Interventions for Families

In the realm of family dynamics, the presence of a narcissist can create a profound and lasting impact. This toxic environment often perpetuates cycles of emotional abuse, leaving family members feeling trapped and powerless. Breaking this cycle requires a multifaceted approach that emphasizes awareness, education, and proactive intervention. Families must first recognize the patterns of behavior that characterize narcissistic relationships, understanding that these patterns are not merely personal faults but can be deeply ingrained manifestations of a personality disorder. By acknowledging these behaviors, families can begin to shift their perceptions and responses, paving the way for healing.

Effective communication serves as the cornerstone of intervention. Encouraging open dialogue among family members allows individuals to express their feelings and experiences without fear of judgment or retaliation. This process fosters emotional intelligence, enabling family members to articulate their needs and boundaries clearly. It is essential to create a safe space where each person's voice is heard and validated. Through active listening and empathetic engagement, families can dismantle the walls erected by narcissistic behavior, fostering a climate of trust and understanding that is crucial for recovery.

Education plays a pivotal role in breaking the cycle of narcissistic abuse. By raising awareness about narcissistic personality disorder and its symptoms, families can better understand the behavior of the narcissist and its impact on their lives. Workshops, support groups, and literature focused on emotional health can provide valuable insights, empowering family members to recognize red flags and develop coping mechanisms. Knowledge equips individuals with the tools needed to navigate the complexities of their relationships, fostering resilience and emotional regulation in the face of ongoing challenges.

Interventions often require external support to reinforce healing efforts within the family. Therapy, whether individual or family-based, can provide a structured environment to explore the emotional scars left by narcissistic abuse. Professional guidance helps families establish healthier dynamics and learn effective strategies for conflict resolution. Support groups also offer a sense of community, allowing survivors to share their experiences and draw strength from one another. By building a robust support system, families can fortify their resolve to break free from the toxic patterns that have long held them captive.

Breaking the cycle of narcissistic abuse is a journey of empowerment and transformation. Families that commit to understanding the intricacies of narcissism and actively work towards healthier relational patterns can create a legacy of emotional intelligence and resilience. This commitment not only fosters healing for current members but also sets a powerful precedent for future generations. By choosing to confront the toxicity head-on, families can cultivate an environment where love, respect, and emotional well-being flourish, allowing them to thrive in the absence of the narcissist's shadow.

Breaking the cycle of narcissistic abuse begins with self-awareness and self-compassion. By recognizing the patterns of manipulation and prioritizing your own well-being, you can create healthy boundaries and build fulfilling relationships.

NARCISSISTIC PARENTS

Understanding the Narcissistic Parent

Understanding the narcissistic parent is a crucial step in unraveling the complexities of narcissism and its profound impact on individuals. At the core of this dynamic lies a fundamental lack of empathy, which manifests in various ways. Narcissistic parents often prioritize their own needs and desires over those of their children, leading to a distorted family structure where the child becomes an extension of the parent's ego. This relationship can create emotional landscapes filled with confusion, self-doubt, and a yearning for validation that may never come. Understanding this dynamic allows adults to recognize the patterns that shaped their upbringing and how these patterns continue to influence their lives.

Narcissistic parents often exhibit traits that align with both grandiose and vulnerable narcissism. The grandiose narcissist may present themselves as highly successful and demanding, often putting immense pressure on their children to achieve perfection. In contrast, the vulnerable narcissist may appear insecure and overly sensitive, yet they still manipulate their children's emotions to maintain control. Both types, however, share a common thread: a deep-seated need for admiration and a profound inability to nurture their children's emotional needs. Identifying these traits is essential for adults seeking to understand their childhood experiences and the emotional toll they may have endured.

Cultural influences play a significant role in shaping the behaviors of narcissistic parents. In societies that emphasize individualism and success, these traits can be magnified, leading parents to adopt a more narcissistic approach to parenting. This environment can create a perfect storm for children who must navigate the high expectations placed upon them. Understanding the cultural context of narcissism can empower adults to recognize that their experiences are not isolated but rather part of a broader societal narrative. This awareness fosters a sense of solidarity and validation, helping individuals reclaim their narratives and break free from cycles of emotional manipulation.

Healing from the impacts of a narcissistic parent requires a profound understanding of one's own emotional landscape. Adults who have grown up under the shadow of a narcissistic parent often struggle with self-worth and boundaries. However, recognizing the signs of emotional manipulation and the patterns of narcissistic behavior can lead to empowerment. By implementing strategies such as setting firm boundaries, seeking therapy, and engaging in supportive communities, individuals can embark on a healing journey. This process not only involves reclaiming one's identity but also cultivating resilience and self-compassion that were often stifled during childhood.

Ultimately, understanding the narcissistic parent is about more than just recognizing harmful behaviors; it is about fostering growth and resilience. By illuminating the traits and patterns associated with narcissistic parenting, adults can gain insight into their own experiences and begin to build healthier relationships. This journey may be challenging, but it is also profoundly rewarding. Embracing the path toward healing allows individuals to break free from the constraints of their past and create a future defined by authenticity, empathy, and genuine connection.

You have the power to rewrite your story.
You have the power to break free from the chains of the past and create a life filled with love, joy, and authentic connection.

Impact on Children

Children who grow up in environments influenced by narcissistic behavior often face unique challenges that profoundly shape their emotional development and self-perception. The pervasive traits of narcissism, such as entitlement, lack of empathy, and an excessive need for admiration, create an atmosphere that is not conducive to healthy emotional growth. Instead of fostering a sense of safety and acceptance, a narcissistic parent may inadvertently instill insecurity and self-doubt in their children. This can lead to a lifetime of struggles with self-esteem and an internalized sense of unworthiness, as the child learns to prioritize their parent's emotional needs over their own.

As these children navigate their formative years, they often become adept at reading the emotional landscape of their narcissistic parent, developing a heightened sensitivity to the moods and whims of those around them. This hyper-awareness can lead to an inability to assert their own needs or desires, resulting in a pattern of people-pleasing that may follow them into adulthood. The constant quest for validation from a narcissistic parent can leave deep psychological scars, making it difficult for the individual to establish healthy boundaries in relationships and fostering an ongoing fear of rejection or abandonment.

Moreover, the impact of narcissism extends beyond the immediate parent-child dynamic. Children of narcissists often struggle to form meaningful connections with peers, as they may lack the social skills necessary to engage authentically. Their experiences of emotional manipulation and conditional love can create barriers to trust and intimacy, leading to loneliness and isolation. In romantic relationships, they may replicate the patterns they learned in childhood, gravitating towards partners who embody similar narcissistic traits or, conversely, becoming overly accommodating in an attempt to avoid conflict.

The effects of growing up in a narcissistic environment can also manifest in mental health challenges. Many children raised by narcissistic parents develop anxiety, depression, or other mood disorders as they grapple with their tumultuous upbringing. These mental health struggles can become intertwined with their identity, making it crucial for individuals to seek therapeutic interventions that address both the trauma of their childhood and the ongoing ramifications in their adult lives. Understanding the emotional landscape shaped by narcissism is essential for healing and reclaiming one's sense of self.

Ultimately, recognizing the impact of narcissism on children is the first step towards breaking the cycle. By fostering awareness and understanding, adults can create supportive environments that prioritize emotional health and resilience. Encouraging open communication and validating feelings can empower individuals to reclaim their identities and cultivate healthier relationships. Healing from the effects of narcissism is not only possible but can lead to profound personal growth, allowing those affected to lead fulfilling lives rich with authentic connections and self-acceptance.

Strategies for Healthy Parenting

Healthy parenting is an essential foundation for nurturing resilient and emotionally intelligent children, particularly when navigating the complexities of narcissism. To foster a positive environment, parents should prioritize open communication, ensuring that their children feel valued and heard. This can be achieved by actively listening to their concerns and validating their feelings, which helps children develop a strong sense of self-worth. By encouraging dialogue, parents can also instill critical thinking skills, enabling their children to differentiate between healthy and unhealthy relationships as they grow.

1. Setting boundaries is another crucial strategy for healthy parenting, especially when dealing with narcissistic influences. Parents must model appropriate boundaries and teach their children the importance of respecting their own limits and those of others. This involves guiding them in recognizing the signs of emotional manipulation and helping them understand that it is acceptable to assert their needs. By reinforcing the idea that boundaries are a vital aspect of any relationship, parents can empower their children to cultivate healthier connections in the future.
2. Self-care is an often-overlooked aspect of parenting that significantly impacts the family dynamic. Parents who prioritize their mental and emotional well-being are better equipped to support their children. Engaging in self-care practices, such as mindfulness, exercise, and seeking professional guidance when necessary, can help parents manage stress and model healthy coping strategies. This awareness not only enhances their parenting skills but also creates a nurturing environment where children can learn the importance of self-care and emotional regulation.
3. Another effective strategy is fostering empathy and emotional intelligence in children. Parents can teach their children to recognize and understand their emotions and those of others, promoting compassion and connection. This can be achieved through discussions about feelings, role-playing scenarios, and encouraging acts of kindness. By nurturing these qualities, parents can help their children build strong interpersonal skills

that will serve them well in all areas of life, including navigating relationships with narcissistic individuals.

4. Lastly, education about narcissism is vital for helping children develop a profound understanding of the complexities of human behavior. By discussing the various types of narcissism and their traits, parents can prepare their children to recognize harmful patterns in themselves and others. This knowledge empowers children to make informed choices about their relationships, equipping them with the tools to either distance themselves from toxic influences or engage in healthier interactions. Ultimately, these strategies foster resilience and emotional strength, preparing children to thrive in a world where narcissism can manifest in many forms.

HEALING FROM NARCISSISTIC ABUSE

Techniques for Recovery

Recovering from the insidious effects of a relationship with a narcissist requires a multifaceted approach that addresses both emotional healing and personal growth. One of the most powerful techniques for recovery is the practice of self-compassion. Understanding that the trauma inflicted by a narcissist is not a reflection of your worth is essential. By nurturing a kind and forgiving inner dialogue, individuals can begin to dismantle the negative self-beliefs that often take root after such experiences. This gentle approach allows survivors to recognize their intrinsic value and rebuild their self-esteem, forming a solid foundation for moving forward.

COGNITIVE RESTRUCTURING Another effective technique is engaging in cognitive restructuring, which involves challenging and reframing negative thought patterns. Survivors of narcissistic abuse frequently grapple with feelings of shame, guilt, and self-doubt. By consciously identifying these detrimental thoughts and replacing them with more empowering beliefs, individuals can shift their perspective. This process not only aids in healing but also fosters resilience, enabling survivors to face future challenges with a renewed sense of strength and clarity. Emphasizing the importance of positive affirmations and realistic self-talk can significantly enhance this technique, helping individuals to redefine their narratives.

MINDFULNESS PRACTICES are also invaluable in the recovery journey. Techniques such as meditation, deep breathing exercises, and grounding activities help individuals reconnect with their emotions and develop greater emotional regulation. By learning to observe their thoughts without judgment, survivors can create a safe mental space where healing can occur. This awareness cultivates a deeper understanding of one's emotional responses, paving the way for healthier coping mechanisms and more balanced emotional management. Mindfulness not only aids in processing trauma but also empowers individuals to live in the present moment, free from the shadows of past pain.

SUPPORT GROUPS, THERAPY, and trusted friends or family members can play a significant role in the healing process. Sharing experiences and insights fosters a sense of community and belonging, which is vital for emotional recovery. Additionally, engaging with professionals who specialize in trauma and narcissistic abuse can offer guidance tailored to individual needs, ensuring that the recovery journey is both informed and supported.

UNDERSTANDING THE DYNAMICS of narcissistic behavior and recognizing the red flags in relationships can help individuals avoid similar situations in the future. Knowledge equips survivors with the skills to navigate their emotional landscapes and enhances their emotional intelligence. This understanding not only aids in personal recovery but also fosters healthier interactions and relationships moving forward. By embracing these techniques, individuals can reclaim their lives, transforming pain into a pathway for growth and resilience.

Emotional Regulation: Tools for Managing Trauma Responses

Emotional regulation is a crucial skill for anyone navigating the tumultuous waters of trauma responses, especially for those who have experienced the insidious effects of narcissistic abuse. Understanding that emotional responses are often rooted in past experiences allows individuals to approach their feelings with compassion rather than judgment. Tools for managing these responses can transform overwhelming emotions into manageable experiences, paving the way for healing and personal growth. By cultivating emotional awareness, survivors can begin to reclaim their narrative and break free from the shackles of past trauma.

1. One effective tool for emotional regulation is mindfulness. This practice encourages individuals to observe their thoughts and feelings without becoming entangled in them. By grounding oneself in the present moment, it becomes easier to recognize when trauma responses are triggered. Mindfulness techniques,

such as deep breathing exercises or guided meditations, can help individuals create a safe mental space, allowing them to process emotions rather than react impulsively. This conscious pause can be empowering, promoting a sense of control that may have been lost in the chaos of a toxic relationship.

2. Another valuable strategy is journaling. Writing about one's thoughts and feelings can serve as a powerful outlet for emotional expression. This practice not only allows survivors to articulate their experiences but also helps in identifying patterns and triggers associated with trauma responses. By putting pen to paper, individuals can explore their emotions in a structured way, leading to insights that can facilitate healing. Journaling also provides a record of progress, enabling survivors to celebrate their growth and resilience over time.

3. Support groups can be instrumental in the journey of emotional regulation. Connecting with others who have faced similar challenges offers a sense of belonging and understanding that is often missing in the aftermath of narcissistic abuse. Sharing experiences in a safe environment can validate feelings and foster emotional resilience. These groups can also provide practical tools and coping mechanisms that have proven effective for others, enhancing the collective healing process. Building a community of support not only aids in emotional regulation but reinforces the idea that survivors are not alone in their struggles.

4. Finally, cultivating self-compassion is essential for effective emotional regulation. Survivors of narcissistic abuse often grapple with guilt and shame, believing they should have acted differently or avoided their circumstances. By practicing self-kindness and recognizing that trauma responses are natural reactions to harmful experiences, individuals can foster a

healthier relationship with themselves. Engaging in positive self-talk and affirmations can gradually shift negative thought patterns, instilling a sense of worthiness and hope. Embracing this journey of self-discovery and emotional management empowers survivors to navigate their healing with grace and resilience, ultimately leading to a brighter, more fulfilling future.

EMPOWERMENT THROUGH EDUCATION

Raising Awareness about Narcissism

Raising awareness about narcissism is a crucial step in fostering understanding and healing for those affected by toxic relationships. Narcissism, often cloaked in charm and charisma, can lead to devastating emotional and psychological consequences. By educating ourselves and others about the characteristics and behaviors associated with narcissistic personality disorder, we can empower individuals to recognize the signs and take action before falling into the trap of manipulation and control. Awareness is the first line of defense in combating the insidious nature of narcissistic abuse, enabling victims to reclaim their power and begin the journey toward recovery.

Understanding the symptoms and diagnostic criteria of narcissistic personality disorder is essential for identifying toxic dynamics in relationships. Many adults may not realize that their experiences of emotional manipulation, gaslighting, and emotional neglect are rooted in narcissistic behavior. By shining a light on these behaviors, we can help individuals distinguish between healthy and unhealthy relationships.

This knowledge not only fosters emotional intelligence but also cultivates a community that supports victims in sharing their experiences without shame or fear, allowing for collective healing and understanding.

The impact of narcissism extends beyond individual relationships, affecting family dynamics and creating cycles of abuse that can persist across generations. When we raise awareness about the pervasive nature of narcissism, we highlight the importance of breaking these cycles. Families can learn to recognize red flags and transform toxic patterns into healthier interactions. Empowering individuals with knowledge about narcissism can lead to healthier communication, stronger boundaries, and ultimately, more fulfilling relationships. By prioritizing emotional intelligence, we can foster environments where empathy and understanding thrive, paving the way for healing and growth.

Coping mechanisms for survivors of narcissistic abuse are vital components of recovery. Raising awareness provides survivors with tools to manage trauma responses effectively and develop emotional regulation strategies. Survivors often grapple with feelings of worthlessness and confusion after enduring narcissistic manipulation, making it imperative to create supportive networks where they can share their experiences and learn from one another. Educational initiatives that promote understanding and compassion can transform the stigma surrounding narcissistic abuse into a collective movement toward healing and empowerment.

Finally, the journey toward healing from narcissistic abuse begins with education and awareness. By illuminating the reality of narcissism and its impact, we create a space for survivors to feel validated and understood. This awareness not only serves to protect potential victims but also encourages those who have suffered to embark on their healing journeys with courage. As we foster emotional intelligence and resilience, we equip individuals with the tools they need to navigate their relationships with confidence, ensuring that they can build healthier, more fulfilling connections in the future.

MOVING FORWARD

Steps Towards Empowerment

Empowerment begins with awareness, a crucial first step in reclaiming one's life from the clutches of a narcissistic relationship. Understanding the traits and behaviors of narcissists allows individuals to recognize patterns that may have previously gone unnoticed. This awareness serves as a powerful tool, illuminating the red flags that signify toxic dynamics. By educating oneself about narcissistic personality disorder and its impact, individuals can shift their perspective from self-blame to understanding, paving the way for healing. Knowledge empowers survivors to set boundaries and make informed decisions about their relationships moving forward.

The journey towards empowerment also involves cultivating emotional intelligence. This essential skill enables individuals to navigate their emotions and respond to challenging situations with clarity and resilience. Developing emotional intelligence involves practicing self-awareness, self-regulation, empathy, and effective communication. Each of these components contributes to healthier interactions with oneself and others. As survivors learn to identify and manage their emotional responses, they begin to break free from the cycle of abuse, fostering a sense of autonomy and control over their lives.

Surrounding oneself with understanding and compassionate individuals creates a safe space for healing and growth. Support groups, therapy, and trusted friends can provide validation and encouragement, allowing survivors to share their experiences without fear of judgment. This sense of community reinforces the idea that they are not alone in their struggles, making it easier to process their trauma and rebuild their self-esteem. The journey of recovery is not meant to be undertaken in isolation; it is through connection that individuals find strength and resilience.

In addition to support, developing practical coping mechanisms can significantly enhance one's empowerment. Techniques such as mindfulness, journaling, and creative expression allow survivors to process their emotions and experiences in healthy ways. These methods serve as outlets for stress and anxiety, helping to regulate emotional responses and promote healing. Establishing routines that prioritize self-care is equally important, as nurturing oneself physically, emotionally, and mentally lays the foundation for long-term recovery. Empowerment flourishes when individuals actively engage in their healing process, taking proactive steps toward reclaiming their lives.

Ultimately, empowerment is about reclaiming one's narrative and embracing the journey of self-discovery. It involves recognizing the strength that resides within, even after experiencing the devastating effects of narcissistic abuse. As individuals learn to trust themselves and their instincts, they cultivate a sense of purpose and direction. Embracing personal growth and transformation fosters a renewed sense of identity, allowing survivors to emerge from the shadows of toxic relationships with newfound confidence. This empowerment enables them not only to heal but also to inspire others, spreading awareness and promoting emotional health in their communities.

Building Healthy Relationships Post-Abuse

Building healthy relationships post-abuse is a transformative journey that requires courage, patience, and a commitment to personal growth. Survivors of narcissistic abuse often carry emotional scars that can misalign their perceptions of love and trust. However, this period of healing presents a unique opportunity to redefine what a healthy relationship looks like. By prioritizing emotional intelligence and self-awareness, individuals can cultivate connections that are nurturing and supportive, breaking free from the patterns of toxicity that have previously defined their experiences.

The first step in building healthy relationships is to understand and acknowledge the trauma endured. It is essential to engage in self-reflection, allowing oneself to process past experiences and their impact on emotional well-being. This involves recognizing the red flags that characterized previous relationships and committing to avoiding similar dynamics in the future. By identifying these patterns, survivors can develop a clearer understanding of their emotional needs and boundaries, which are crucial for establishing connections that foster mutual respect and understanding.

Developing skills in emotional regulation and empathy enhances one's ability to connect authentically with others. This means not only understanding one's feelings but also being attuned to the emotions of others. By practicing active listening and cultivating compassion, individuals can create a safe space for vulnerability and open communication. These foundational elements are vital in nurturing relationships that prioritize emotional safety, allowing both partners to express their needs and feelings without fear of judgment or retaliation.

As relationships begin to flourish, it is important to establish boundaries that safeguard emotional health. Healthy relationships are built on mutual respect, and each individual must feel empowered to voice their concerns and needs. These boundaries are not walls but rather guidelines that promote understanding and accountability. They serve as a means to protect oneself from the potential recurrence of toxic dynamics. By fostering an environment where both partners can thrive, a solid foundation for a resilient relationship can be established.

Finally, seeking support from trusted friends, family, or professional counselors can be invaluable in the journey toward building healthy relationships. Engaging with a community that understands the complexities of narcissistic abuse can provide encouragement, validation, and shared experiences that ease the healing process. Empowerment through education about narcissism and emotional health is key to breaking the cycle of abuse. As survivors embrace their journey with resilience, they can inspire others to seek the love and connection they deserve, ultimately transforming their pain into a beacon of hope for themselves and those around them.

Embracing Your Journey

Embracing your journey is a pivotal step in reclaiming your life after the turmoil of narcissistic abuse. The road may be fraught with challenges, but it also holds the promise of profound personal growth. As you navigate through the emotional wreckage, it is essential to recognize that your experiences do not define you. Instead, they serve as the backdrop for a powerful narrative of resilience and recovery. Acknowledging the pain is the first step toward healing; it is an essential part of your journey to understanding the trauma bond and how it has shaped your perspective.

Treat yourself with the same compassion and urgency you would extend to someone recovering from a physical injury. This mindset allows you to prioritize self-care and seek the necessary support, whether through therapy, support groups, or self-help resources. Healing from PTSD is not a linear path; it is often filled with setbacks and breakthroughs. Embrace each moment as a vital part of your recovery.

Breaking free from the toxic patterns established by a narcissistic relationship is both challenging and liberating. Understanding the dynamics of trauma bonds can illuminate why you may feel tethered to your past. This knowledge can empower you to dismantle those connections and foster healthier relationships with yourself and others. As you navigate the complexities of emotional healing, consider setting boundaries that honor your needs. Each boundary you establish allows you to reclaim a piece of your identity, reinforcing your sense of self-worth and autonomy.

The aftermath of narcissistic abuse can often lead to feelings of despair and hopelessness. However, embracing your journey also means recognizing the potential for post-traumatic growth. This concept emphasizes that even in the darkest times, there lies an opportunity to emerge stronger and more resilient. By actively engaging in your healing process, you can cultivate new strengths and insights that transform your life. Celebrate the small victories along the way, whether it's a day free from intrusive thoughts or the courage to express your feelings. Each step forward is a testament to your strength and determination.

Ultimately, embracing your journey is about reclaiming your narrative. You have the power to redefine your story, turning the pain of the past into a source of inspiration for a brighter future. It is vital to remember that healing is not a destination but a lifelong process. Surround yourself with supportive individuals who uplift and encourage you. Engage in activities that nourish your spirit and foster joy. Your journey through the aftermath of narcissistic abuse may be filled with challenges, but it is also a path toward self-discovery and empowerment. Embrace it wholeheartedly, knowing that you are not alone and that brighter days lie ahead.

Inspiring Others Through Your Story

In the journey of healing from the chaos of narcissistic abuse, sharing your personal story can serve as a beacon of hope for others. Your experiences, no matter how painful, possess the power to inspire those still trapped in the cycle of trauma. When you articulate your struggles, you validate the feelings of others who may feel isolated and misunderstood. This connection fosters a sense of community, reminding individuals that they are not alone in their battles. By owning your narrative, you not only empower yourself but also encourage others to confront their own pain and seek the light that lies beyond.

Every tale of survival is a testament to resilience. As you recount your journey, emphasize the moments of strength that emerged from vulnerability. Highlighting the transformation from victimhood to empowerment can resonate deeply with those grappling with their own trauma bonds. Your story can illustrate that healing is not linear and that setbacks can coexist with triumphs. This duality is essential in helping others understand that they, too, can navigate their path toward recovery, finding solace in the knowledge that growth often arises from adversity.

Moreover, sharing your story can demystify the complexities of PTSD and the emotional aftermath of narcissistic relationships. By framing PTSD as an injury rather than a disorder, you pave the way for a more compassionate understanding of mental health. This perspective encourages individuals to seek treatment and view their struggles as a legitimate concern that requires care and attention. When you articulate your healing journey, you not only advocate for yourself but also for others who may feel ashamed or stigmatized by their experiences. Your voice can challenge societal misconceptions, fostering a culture of empathy and support.

Inspiration often lies in actionable insights. As you narrate your story, weave in the coping mechanisms and strategies that have supported your recovery. Whether it be through therapy, mindfulness practices, or community support, sharing practical tools empowers others to take proactive steps in their healing. Your journey can serve as a roadmap, illustrating that while the path may be fraught with challenges, there are tangible ways to navigate the chaos. Highlighting these strategies fosters a sense of agency and hope, encouraging others to reclaim their lives.

Ultimately, your story is a powerful reminder that growth is possible after trauma. By sharing your narrative, you not only inspire others to confront their own challenges but also cultivate a sense of solidarity within the community of survivors. Your experiences can ignite a spark of courage in those who feel hopeless, urging them to explore their own paths toward healing. As you speak your truth, you contribute to a larger dialogue about resilience, recovery, and the profound strength found in vulnerability, making a lasting impact on those who need it most.

Embrace your journey,
celebrate your progress,
and remember that you are worthy
of love and happiness!

Healing from narcissistic abuse is not just about surviving, it's about thriving. It's about reclaiming your power, rewriting your story, and living a life filled with joy, authenticity, and purpose.

This Book is Informed by a Comprehensive Foundation of Research in Psychology, Clinical Therapy, and Trauma Coaching.

www.ingramcontent.com/pod-product-compliance
Lightning Source LLC
LaVergne TN
LVHW050933210926
848482LV00013B/603
* 9 7 9 8 3 4 8 5 0 2 6 9 0 *